The
AFTERNOON TEA
Collection

STERLING
New York

An Imprint of Sterling Publishing
387 Park Avenue South
New York, NY 10016

This 2013 edition published by Sterling Publishing by arrangement with ACP Books.

ISBN 978-1-4549-1019-0

Distributed in Canada by Sterling Publishing
c/o Canadian Manda Group, 165 Dufferin Street
Toronto, Ontario, Canada M6K 3H6

For information about custom editions, special sales, and premium and corporate purchases,
please contact Sterling Special Sales at 800-805-5489 or specialsales@sterlingpublishing.com.

Manufactured in China

2 4 6 8 10 9 7 5 3 1

www.sterlingpublishing.com

The
AFTERNOON TEA
Collection

STERLING
New York

Contents

The teatime experience

Afternoon tea is a celebration of all things delightful and delectable, pretty and feminine. Set the table with a white tablecloth, fine china teacups, polished silverware and simply arranged flowers. The tiered serving stand is an essential accoutrement. Laden with little sandwiches, scones, pastries and tarts it is the centerpiece of the table, and the pièce de résistance of the teatime experience. And when the doorbell rings, it's time to put the kettle on.

Sandwiches

Afternoon tea always starts with sandwiches. Usually they're little finger sandwiches with the crusts cut off and a simple subtle filling, but they can also be cut into triangles. Make sure you don't overfill tea sandwiches – they should be delicate and one or two mouthfuls only.

chicken and almond sandwiches

1 cup chicken stock
1 cup water
6 black peppercorns
1 bay leaf
8 ounces chicken breast
1 stalk celery, trimmed, chopped finely
2 tablespoons flaked almonds, roasted
¼ cup crème fraîche
2 tablespoons whole-egg mayonnaise
1 teaspoon lemon juice
2 teaspoons finely chopped fresh tarragon
1 ounce butter, softened
8 slices light rye bread

1 Combine stock, the water, peppercorns, bay leaf and chicken in small saucepan; bring to the boil. Reduce heat; simmer, uncovered, about 15 minutes or until chicken is cooked through, turning chicken halfway through cooking time. Remove chicken from poaching liquid. When cool enough to handle, chop chicken finely.

2 Combine chicken in medium bowl with celery, nuts, crème fraîche, mayonnaise, juice and tarragon. Season to taste.

3 Spread butter over bread slices; top half the slices with chicken mixture then remaining bread. Cut crusts from bread; cut each sandwich into three finger sandwiches, then cut each in half crossways into squares.

prep + cook time
35 minutes (+ cooling)
makes 24

marinated cucumber sandwiches

The cucumber can be sliced
with a vegetable peeler for even,
thin slices.

- 2 lebanese cucumbers, sliced
  thinly lengthways
- 1 tablespoon white wine
  vinegar
- 1 tablespoon finely chopped
  fresh dill
- ½ teaspoon sea salt flakes
- ½ teaspoon superfine sugar
- ¼ teaspoon cracked
  black pepper
- 1 ounce butter, softened
- 8 slices wholemeal bread
- ½ cup crème fraîche

1 Combine cucumber, vinegar,
dill, salt, sugar and pepper in
medium bowl. Cover; refrigerate
2 hours.
2 Drain cucumber; discard
excess liquid.
3 Spread butter over bread
slices. Spread crème fraîche
over half the buttered bread
slices; top slices with cucumber
then remaining bread. Cut crusts
from bread; cut each sandwich
into four fingers.

prep time 20 minutes
(+ refrigeration)
makes 16

curried egg sandwiches

6 hard-boiled eggs,
   chopped coarsely
⅓ cup whole-egg mayonnaise
2 teaspoons curry powder
8 slices white bread
2 cups shredded iceberg
   lettuce

1 Use a fork to mash egg, mayonnaise and curry powder in medium bowl. Season to taste.
2 Spread egg mixture over half the bread slices; top with lettuce then remaining bread. Cut crusts from bread; cut each sandwich into four triangles.

prep time 15 minutes
makes 16

salmon and herbed cream cheese sandwiches

2 ounces cream cheese, softened

2 teaspoons each finely chopped fresh dill and chives

2 teaspoons lemon juice

1 teaspoon drained baby capers, rinsed, chopped finely

4 slices white bread, crusts removed

4 ounces thinly sliced smoked salmon

4 large arugula leaves, trimmed

1 Combine cream cheese, dill, chives, juice and capers in small bowl. Season to taste.

2 Using rolling pin, roll over one slice of bread to flatten slightly. Spread with a quarter of the cream cheese mixture; top with a quarter of the smoked salmon and one arugula leaf, roll tightly to enclose filling. Repeat with remaining bread, cream cheese mixture, smoked salmon and arugula. Trim ends then cut each roll into four pieces.

prep time 20 minutes
makes 16

shrimp and lime pepper aïoli sandwiches

16 cooked medium shrimp
1 ounce butter, softened
8 slices white bread
1 cup shredded baby romaine lettuce

lime pepper aïoli
½ cup whole-egg mayonnaise
1 small clove garlic, crushed
½ teaspoon finely grated lime rind
2 teaspoons lime juice
¼ teaspoon cracked black pepper

1 Make lime pepper aïoli.
2 Shell and devein shrimp; halve lengthways. Stir shrimp into aïoli. Season to taste.
3 Spread butter over bread slices; top half the slices with prawn mixture and shredded lettuce then remaining bread. Cut crusts from bread; cut each sandwich into four triangles.

lime pepper aïoli Combine ingredients in medium bowl.

prep time 25 minutes
makes 16

chicken and celery sandwiches

3 cups finely chopped cooked chicken
4 scallions, chopped finely
½ cup finely chopped roasted walnuts
3 stalks celery, trimmed, chopped finely
½ cup whole-egg mayonnaise
⅓ cup sour cream
20 slices white bread
10 slices wholemeal bread

1 Combine chicken, scallions, nuts, celery, mayonnaise and sour cream in large bowl.

2 Spread half the chicken mixture onto half the white bread slices; top with wholemeal bread slices. Spread remaining chicken mixture onto wholemeal bread then top with remaining white bread slices. Cut crusts from bread; cut each sandwich into three fingers.

prep time 40 minutes
makes 30

Scones

At afternoon teas in country houses the tradition is to put the scones in the oven just as the guests arrive. Warm from the oven and served with jam and cream, fresh scones are an experience not to be missed. This lovely country tradition can be duplicated in your own home – make them no more than an hour before you cook them.

scones with jam and cream

Scones are best made on the day of serving. They can be frozen for up to 3 months. Thaw in oven, wrapped in foil. You could substitute the double cream for clotted cream or whipped thickened cream.

2½ cups self-raising flour
1 tablespoon superfine sugar
1 ounce butter, chopped
1¼ cups buttermilk
¾ cup black cherry jam
1 cup thick cream

1 Preheat oven to 425°F. Grease 9-inch square cake pan.
2 Sift flour and sugar into large bowl; rub in butter.
3 Add buttermilk. Use a knife to cut the buttermilk through the flour mixture to make a soft, sticky dough. Turn dough onto floured surface, knead gently until smooth.
4 Press dough out to ¾-inch thickness, cut out 1½-inch rounds. Place scones, just touching, in pan. Gently knead scraps of dough together; repeat process. Brush scones with a little extra buttermilk.
5 Bake scones about 15 minutes. Serve warm scones with jam and cream.

prep + cook time 35 minutes
makes 25

vanilla bean scones

Scones are best made on the day of serving. They can be frozen for up to 3 months. Thaw in oven, wrapped in foil. It is fine to use just one 10 oz. carton of cream for this recipe.

2½ cups self-raising flour
  1 tablespoon superfine sugar
  1   ounce butter, chopped
  ¾ cup milk
  ½ cup water
  1 vanilla bean
1¼ cups heavy cream
  2 tablespoons confectioners' sugar
  ¾ cup strawberry jam
  8 ounces strawberries, sliced thinly

1 Preheat oven to 425°F. Grease 9-inch square cake pan.
2 Sift flour and superfine sugar into large bowl; rub in butter.
3 Combine milk and the water in a medium jug. Split vanilla bean open and scrape seeds into milk mixture; discard bean. Add milk mixture to flour mixture; use a knife to cut the milk mixture through the flour mixture to make a soft, sticky dough. Turn dough onto floured surface, knead gently until smooth.
4 Press dough out to 8-inch square, cut into 16 squares using floured knife. Place squares, just touching, in pan. Brush scones with a little extra milk.

5 Bake scones about 20 minutes.
6 Meanwhile, beat cream and half the sifted confectioners' sugar in small bowl with electric mixer until soft peaks form.
7 Sandwich warm scones with jam, strawberries and cream; serve dusted with remaining sifted confectioners' sugar.

prep + cook time 40 minutes
makes 16

date scones with whipped caramel butter

Scones are best made on the day of serving. They can be frozen for up to 3 months. Thaw in oven, wrapped in foil.

1 ounce butter, softened
¼ cup firmly packed brown sugar
1 egg yolk
2½ cups self-raising flour
⅓ cup finely chopped seeded dried dates
1¼ cups buttermilk

whipped caramel butter
5 ounces unsalted butter, softened
¼ cup brown sugar
2 teaspoons vanilla extract

1 Preheat oven to 425°F. Grease 9-inch square cake pan.
2 Beat butter, sugar and egg yolk in small bowl with electric mixer until light and fluffy. Transfer mixture to large bowl; add sifted flour, dates and buttermilk. Use a knife to cut the buttermilk through the flour mixture to make a soft, sticky dough. Turn dough onto floured surface, knead gently until smooth.
3 Press dough out to 8-inch square, cut into nine squares, using a floured knife, then cut each square in half diagonally. Place scones side by side, just touching, in pan. Brush scones with a little extra buttermilk.

4 Bake scones about 20 minutes.
5 Meanwhile, make whipped caramel butter.
6 Serve warm scones with whipped caramel butter.

whipped caramel butter Beat ingredients in small bowl with electric mixer until light and fluffy.

prep + cook time 40 minutes
makes 18

gingerbread scones with lemon glacé icing

Scones are best made on the day of serving. They can be frozen for up to 3 months. Thaw in oven, wrapped in foil. Use a zester to shred lemon rind.

1 ounce butter, softened
¼ cup firmly packed light brown sugar
1 egg yolk
2½ cups self-raising flour
3 teaspoons ground ginger
1½ teaspoons ground cinnamon
¼ teaspoon ground cloves
1 cup buttermilk
2 tablespoons treacle or golden syrup

lemon glacé icing
1 cup confectioners' sugar
½ ounce butter, melted
1 tablespoon lemon juice, approximately

1 Preheat oven to 425°F. Grease 9-inch square cake pan.
2 Beat butter, sugar and egg yolk in small bowl with electric mixer until light and fluffy. Transfer mixture to large bowl; add sifted dry ingredients and combined buttermilk and treacle. Use a knife to cut the buttermilk mixture through flour mixture to make a soft, sticky dough. Turn dough onto floured surface, knead gently until smooth.
3 Press dough out to ¾-inch thickness, cut into 2-inch rounds. Place rounds, just touching, in pan. Gently knead scraps of dough together; repeat process. Brush scones with a little extra buttermilk.

4 Bake scones about 20 minutes. Cool 10 minutes.
5 Meanwhile, make lemon glacé icing.
6 Serve warm scones drizzled with icing and decorated with shredded lemon rind, if you like.

lemon glacé icing Sift icing sugar into small heatproof bowl; stir in butter and enough juice to make a thick paste. Place bowl over small saucepan of simmering water; stir until mixture is smooth.

prep + cook time 40 minutes
makes 16

Friands

Essentially little cakes made with egg whites and ground nuts, friands look very impressive on the tea table. There are special friand pans you can buy at kitchenware shops but they work just as well if you make them in muffin pans or patty pans.

orange blossom friands

We used tart molds bought from a supermarket, which came in sets of four. The friand mixture will be fine left to stand at room temperature if you're making the friands in small batches. Alternatively, make 12 friands using 12-hole (½-cup) oval friand pan. Divide mixture into pan holes, bake about 20 minutes.

6 egg whites
6 ounces unsalted butter, melted
2 tablespoons honey
1 tablespoon orange blossom water
1 cup ground almonds
1½ cups confectioners' sugar
½ cup plain (all-purpose) flour
½ cup flaked almonds

honey syrup
2 tablespoons honey
1 tablespoon water
2 teaspoons orange blossom water

1 Preheat oven to 400°F. Grease individual fluted tart molds (1½-tablespoon) with butter. Place on oven tray.
2 Place egg whites in medium bowl; whisk lightly with fork until combined. Add butter, honey, orange blossom water, ground almonds, sifted confectioners' sugar and flour; stir until combined. Half fill the tart molds with mixture; sprinkle with almonds.
3 Bake friands about 12 minutes. Stand friands 5 minutes before turning top-side up onto wire rack to cool. Repeat with remaining mixture and almonds.
4 Meanwhile, make honey syrup.
5 Serve friands drizzled with honey syrup.

honey syrup Combine honey and the water in small saucepan; bring to the boil. Remove from heat; stir in orange blossom water. Cool.

prep + cook time
35 minutes (+ cooling)
makes 28

fig and walnut friands

1¼ cups roasted walnuts
6 egg whites
6 ounces unsalted butter, melted
1½ cups confectioners' sugar
½ cup plain (all-purpose) flour
2 teaspoons finely grated orange rind
1 tablespoon orange juice
4 dried figs, sliced thinly

1 Preheat oven to 400°F. Grease 12-hole (½-cup) oval friand pan.
2 Process nuts until ground finely.
3 Place egg whites in medium bowl; whisk lightly with fork until combined. Add butter, sifted confectioners' sugar and flour, rind, juice and nuts; stir until combined. Divide mixture into pans, top with slices of fig.
4 Bake friands about 20 minutes. Stand friands 5 minutes before turning top-side up onto wire rack to cool. Serve dusted with a little sifted confectioners' sugar.

prep + cook time 35 minutes
makes 12

mandarin and poppy seed friands

Store friands in an airtight container for up to three days.

2 large mandarins
1 tablespoon poppy seeds
6 egg whites
6 ounces butter, melted
1 cup ground almonds
1½ cups confectioners' sugar
½ cup plain (all-purpose) flour

1 Preheat oven to 400°F. Line 12-hole (½-cup) oval friand pan with paper cases.
2 Finely grate rind from mandarins (you will need 2 tablespoons of rind). Juice the mandarins (you will need 2 tablespoons of juice).
3 Combine poppy seeds and juice in small jug; stand 10 minutes.
4 Place egg whites in medium bowl; whisk lightly with fork until combined. Add butter, ground almonds, sifted confectioners' sugar and flour, rind and poppy seed mixture; stir until combined. Divide mixture into paper cases.
5 Bake friands about 20 minutes. Stand friands 5 minutes before turning, top-side up, onto wire rack to cool. Serve lightly dusted with sifted confectioners' sugar.

prep + cook time 35 minutes
makes 12

lemon and cranberry friands

Store friands in an airtight container for up to three days.

6 egg whites
6 ounces butter, melted
1 cup ground almonds
1½ cups confectioners' sugar
½ cup plain (all-purpose) flour
¾ cup dried cranberries
1 tablespoon finely grated lemon rind
1 tablespoon lemon juice

1 Preheat oven to 400°F. Grease 12-hole (½-cup) oval friand pan.
2 Place egg whites in medium bowl; whisk lightly with fork until combined. Add butter, ground almonds, sifted confectioners' sugar and flour, berries, rind and juice; stir until combined. Divide mixture into pan holes.
3 Bake friands about 20 minutes. Stand friands 5 minutes before turning, top-side up, onto wire rack to cool. Serve lightly dusted with sifted confectioners' sugar.

prep + cook time 35 minutes
makes 12

pistachio and lime friands

Store friands in an airtight container for up to three days. We used freeform paper cases made by pushing a 4¾-inch square of paper (we used paper about the same thickness as printer paper) into ungreased pan holes, followed by a 4¾-inch square of parchment paper.

1 cup roasted unsalted pistachios
6 egg whites
6 ounces butter, melted
1½ cups confectioners' sugar
½ cup plain (all-purpose) flour
2 teaspoons finely grated lime rind
1 tablespoon lime juice

1 Preheat oven to 400°F. Line 12-hole (½-cup) oval friand pan.
2 Process nuts until ground finely.
3 Place egg whites in medium bowl; whisk lightly with fork until combined. Add butter, sifted confectioners' sugar and flour, rind, juice and nuts; stir until combined. Divide mixture into pan holes.
4 Bake friands about 25 minutes. Stand friands 5 minutes before turning, top-side up, onto wire rack to cool. Serve dusted with a little sifted confectioners' sugar.

prep + cook time 40 minutes
makes 12

Little Tarts

Little tarts are the prettiest things on the tea table. Custard tarts, fruit tarts, chocolate tarts, lemon tarts – they're all absolutely irresistible. It's wise to make more than you think you'll need – you can be sure there will be none left at the end of teatime.

custard fruit flans

Pastry cases and custard cream can be made and stored separately, two days ahead; fold cream into custard just before using. Assemble and serve flans as close to serving as possible – about an hour is good.

1¾ cups plain (all-purpose) flour
¼ cup confectioners' sugar
6 ounces cold butter, chopped coarsely
1 egg yolk
2 teaspoons iced water, approximately
1 medium kiwifruit
2 ounces fresh raspberries, halved
2 ounces fresh blueberries

custard cream
1 cup milk
1 teaspoon vanilla extract
3 egg yolks
⅓ cup superfine sugar
2 tablespoons pure cornstarch
⅓ cup heavy cream, whipped

1 Process flour, sugar and butter until crumbly. With motor operating, add egg yolk and enough of the water to make ingredients come together. Turn dough onto floured surface, knead gently until smooth. Wrap pastry in plastic; refrigerate 30 minutes.
2 Grease two 12-hole (1-tablespoon) mini muffin pans. Roll out half the pastry between sheets of baking paper until ⅛ inch thick. Cut out 12 x 2¼-inch rounds; press rounds into holes of one pan. Prick bases of cases well with a fork. Repeat with remaining pastry. Refrigerate 30 minutes.
3 Preheat oven to 425°F.
4 Bake cases about 12 minutes. Stand cases 5 minutes before transferring to wire rack to cool.
5 Meanwhile, make custard cream.
6 Cut kiwifruit crossways into eight slices; cut 1¼-inch rounds from slices. Divide custard cream into cases; top with fruit.

custard cream Combine milk and extract in small saucepan; bring to the boil. Meanwhile, beat egg yolks, sugar and cornflour in small bowl with electric mixer until thick. With motor operating, gradually beat in hot milk mixture. Return custard to pan; stir over heat until mixture boils and thickens. Cover surface of custard with plastic wrap, refrigerate 1 hour. Fold cream into custard, in two batches.

prep + cook time
1 hour (+ refrigeration & cooling)
makes 24

limoncello meringue pies

Pastry cases and curd can be made 2 days ahead. Store the cases in an airtight container and the curd in the refrigerator.

- 1¾ cups plain (all-purpose) flour
- ¼ cup confectioners' sugar
- 6 ounces cold unsalted butter, chopped coarsely
- 1 egg yolk
- 2 teaspoons iced water, approximately
- 3 egg whites
- ¾ cup superfine sugar

limoncello curd
- 3 egg yolks
- ½ cup superfine sugar
- 1 teaspoon finely grated lemon rind
- ¼ cup lemon juice
- 3 ounces cold unsalted butter, chopped
- 1 tablespoon limoncello liqueur

1 Make limoncello curd.

2 Process flour, confectioners' sugar and butter until crumbly. With motor operating, add egg yolk and enough of the water to make ingredients come together. Turn dough onto floured surface, knead gently until smooth. Wrap pastry in plastic; refrigerate 30 minutes.

3 Grease two 12-hole (1-tablespoon) mini muffin pans. Roll out half the pastry between sheets of baking paper until ¼ inch thick. Cut out 12 x 2¼-inch rounds; press rounds into holes of one pan. Prick base of cases well with a fork. Repeat with remaining pastry. Refrigerate 30 minutes.

4 Meanwhile, preheat oven to 425°F.

5 Bake cases about 12 minutes. Stand cases 5 minutes before transferring to wire rack to cool.

6 Beat egg whites in small bowl with electric mixer until soft peaks form. Gradually add superfine sugar, beating until dissolved between additions.

7 Increase oven to 475°F.

8 Divide limoncello curd into cases. Spoon meringue mixture into piping bag fitted with ½-inch plain tube; pipe meringue over curd.

9 Bake pies about 2 minutes. Cool.

limoncello curd Whisk egg yolks and sugar in medium heatproof bowl until pale and thickened slightly. Whisk in rind and juice; stir over medium saucepan of simmering water about 12 minutes or until mixture coats the back of a spoon. Remove from heat; gradually whisk in butter until combined between additions. Stir in limoncello; cover, refrigerate overnight.

prep + cook time
1 hour 15 minutes
(+ refrigeration & cooling)
makes 24

cherry bakewell tarts

3 ounces unsalted butter, softened
2 tablespoons superfine sugar
1 egg yolk
1 cup plain (all-purpose) flour
½ cup ground almonds
2 tablespoons strawberry jam
12 red glacé cherries, halved

almond filling

4 ounces unsalted butter, softened
½ teaspoon finely grated lemon rind
½ cup superfine sugar
2 eggs
¾ cup ground almonds
2 tablespoons all-purpose flour

lemon glaze

1 cup confectioners' sugar
2 tablespoons lemon juice, approximately

1 Beat butter, sugar and egg yolk in small bowl with electric mixer until combined. Stir in sifted flour and ground almonds in two batches. Turn dough onto floured surface, knead gently until smooth, wrap in plastic; refrigerate 30 minutes.
2 Preheat oven to 425°F.
3 Make almond filling.
4 Grease two 12-hole (1½-tablespoons) shallow round-based patty pans. Roll pastry between sheets of baking paper until ⅛ inch thick. Cut 24 x 2¼-inch rounds from pastry; gently press rounds into holes in pans. Spoon jam then filling into cases.
5 Bake tarts about 20 minutes. Stand tarts 10 minutes; turn, top-side up, onto wire rack.
6 Meanwhile, make lemon glaze.
7 Spoon glaze over warm tarts; top with cherries. Cool.

almond filling Beat butter, rind and sugar in small bowl with electric mixer until light and fluffy. Beat in eggs, one at a time. Stir in ground almonds and flour.

lemon glaze Sift confectioners' sugar into small bowl, stir in enough juice to make glaze pourable.

prep + cook time
1 hour (+ refrigeration & cooling)
makes 24

neenish and pineapple tarts

1¾ cups plain (all-purpose) flour
¼ cup confectioners' sugar
6 ounces cold butter, chopped coarsely
1 egg yolk
2 teaspoons iced water, approximately
2 tablespoons strawberry jam
2 tablespoons finely chopped glacé pineapple

mock cream

¾ cup superfine sugar
1½ tablespoons milk
⅓ cup water
½ teaspoon gelatin
6 ounces unsalted butter, softened
1 teaspoon vanilla extract

glacé icing

1½ cups confectioners' sugar
½ ounce unsalted butter, melted
2 tablespoons hot milk, approximately
yellow and pink food coloring
½ teaspoon cocoa powder

1 Process flour, sugar and butter until crumbly. With motor operating, add egg yolk and enough of the water to make ingredients come together. Turn dough onto floured surface, knead gently until smooth. Wrap pastry in plastic; refrigerate 30 minutes.
2 Grease two 12-hole (2-tablespoons) deep flat-based patty pans. Roll out half the pastry between sheets of baking paper until ⅛ inch thick. Cut out 12 x 3-inch rounds; press rounds into holes of one pan. Prick bases of cases well with a fork. Repeat with remaining pastry. Refrigerate 30 minutes.
3 Preheat oven to 425°F.
4 Bake cases about 12 minutes. Stand cases 5 minutes before transferring to wire rack to cool.
5 Meanwhile, make mock cream and glacé icing.
6 Divide jam among half the cases and pineapple among remaining cases. Fill cases with mock cream, level tops with spatula. Spread yellow icing over pineapple tarts. Spread pink icing over half of each jam tart; spread remaining half with chocolate icing.

mock cream Stir sugar, milk and ¼ cup of the water in small saucepan over low heat, without boiling, until sugar dissolves. Sprinkle gelatin over remaining water in small jug; stir into milk mixture until gelatin dissolves. Cool to room temperature. Beat butter and extract in small bowl with electric mixer until as white as possible. With motor operating, gradually beat in cold milk mixture; beat until light and fluffy.

glacé icing Sift icing sugar into medium bowl; stir in butter and enough of the milk to make a thick paste. Place ⅔ cup of the icing in small heatproof bowl; tint with yellow coloring. Divide remaining icing between two small heatproof bowls; tint icing in one bowl with pink coloring and the other with sifted cocoa. Stir each bowl over small saucepan of simmering water until icing is spreadable.

prep + cook time
1 hour 10 minutes
(+ refrigeration & cooling)
makes 24

rhubarb frangipane tarts

1 vanilla bean
½ cup superfine sugar
¼ cup water
10 stalks trimmed rhubarb, cut
   into 1½-inch lengths
1½ ounces butter, softened
2 tablespoons superfine sugar,
   extra
½ teaspoon vanilla extract
1 egg yolk
½ cup ground almonds
2 teaspoons plain (all-purpose)
   flour
1 sheet butter puff pastry

1 Preheat oven to 350°F. Grease two oven trays.
2 Split vanilla bean, scrape seeds into a small saucepan; discard bean. Add sugar and the water to the pan. Stir syrup over heat, without boiling, until sugar dissolves. Combine rhubarb and syrup in medium baking dish; bake, uncovered, 15 minutes or until rhubarb is tender. Cool. Drain rhubarb; reserve syrup.
3 Meanwhile, beat butter, extra sugar, extract and egg yolk in small bowl with electric mixer until light and fluffy. Stir in ground almonds and flour.

4 Cut pastry into quarters; cut each quarter into three rectangles. Place pastry rectangles about 2 inches apart on trays; spread rounded teaspoons of almond mixture over each rectangle, leaving a ¼-inch border. Top with rhubarb; fold pastry edges in towards center to form raised border.
5 Bake tarts about 25 minutes. Serve tarts warm, brushed with reserved syrup.

prep + cook time
1 hour 10 minutes (+ cooling)
makes 12

passionfruit curd and coconut tarts

1¾ cups plain (all-purpose) flour
¼ cup confectioners' sugar
¼ cup desiccated coconut
6 ounces cold unsalted butter, chopped coarsely
1 egg yolk
2 teaspoons iced water, approximately
1 small coconut

passionfruit curd

⅓ cup passionfruit pulp
½ cup superfine sugar
2 eggs, beaten lightly
4 ounces unsalted butter, chopped coarsely

1 Make passionfruit curd.

2 Process flour, sugar, desiccated coconut and butter until crumbly. With motor operating, add egg yolk and enough of the water to make ingredients come together. Turn dough onto floured surface, knead gently until smooth. Wrap pastry in plastic; refrigerate 30 minutes.

3 Grease two 12-hole (2-tablespoon) deep flat-based patty pans. Roll out half the pastry between sheets of baking paper until ¼ inch thick. Cut out 12 x 3-inch rounds; press rounds into holes of one pan. Prick bases of cases well with a fork. Repeat with remaining pastry. Refrigerate 30 minutes.

4 Preheat oven to 425°F.

5 Bake cases about 12 minutes or until browned. Stand cases 5 minutes before transferring to wire rack to cool.

6 Increase oven to 475°F. Pierce one eye of the coconut using sharp knife; drain liquid from coconut. Place coconut on oven tray; bake about 10 minutes or until cracks appear. Carefully split the coconut open by hitting with a hammer; remove flesh. Using vegetable peeler, slice coconut into curls; reserve ½ cup coconut curls for this recipe and keep remaining for another use. Roast reserved coconut on oven tray about 5 minutes or until lightly browned.

7 Divide passionfruit curd into cases; top with coconut curls.

passionfruit curd Stir ingredients in medium heatproof bowl over medium saucepan of simmering water about 10 minutes or until mixture coats the back of a wooden spoon. Cover surface with plastic wrap; refrigerate overnight.

prep + cook time
1 hour 10 minutes
(+ refrigeration & cooling)
makes 24

portuguese custard tarts

Make tarts ahead (day before). Store in an airtight container. Re-crisp in 425°F oven for 5 minutes.

- ½ cup superfine sugar
- 2 tablespoons cornstarch
- 3 egg yolks
- ¾ cup milk
- ½ cup light cream
- 1 vanilla bean
- 2-inch strip lemon rind
- 1 sheet butter puff pastry

1 Preheat oven to 425°F. Grease two 12-hole (1-tablespoon) mini muffin pans.
2 Combine sugar and cornstarch in medium saucepan. Gradually whisk in combined egg yolks, milk and cream to make custard.
3 Split vanilla bean, scrape seeds into custard; discard bean. Add rind; stir over heat until mixture comes to the boil. Strain custard into medium jug. Cover surface of custard with plastic while making pastry cases.

4 Cut pastry sheet in half; place the two halves on top of each other. Roll pastry up tightly from long side; cut log into 24 rounds. Roll each pastry round on floured surface until 2¼ inches in diameter. Press pastry rounds into pan holes.
5 Divide custard between cases.
6 Bake tarts about 12 minutes. Turn tarts top-side up onto wire rack to cool. Dust with a little sifted icing sugar before serving, if you like.

prep + cook time 45 minutes
makes 24

lemon crème brûlée tarts

Blowtorches are available from kitchenware and hardware stores. It is fine to use just one 10 oz. carton of cream for this recipe.

1¼ cups pouring cream
⅓ cup milk
4 x 2-inch strips lemon rind
4 egg yolks
¼ cup superfine sugar

pastry

1¾ cups plain (all-purpose) flour
¼ cup confectioners' sugar
2 teaspoons finely grated lemon rind
6 ounces cold butter, chopped coarsely
1 egg yolk
2 teaspoons iced water, approximately

toffee

1 cup superfine sugar
½ cup water

1 Make pastry.
2 Grease two 12-hole (1½-tablespoon) shallow round-based patty pans. Roll half the pastry between sheets of baking paper to ⅛-inch thickness. Cut out 12 x 2¼-inch fluted rounds; press rounds into pan holes. Prick bases of cases well with a fork. Repeat with remaining pastry. Refrigerate 30 minutes.
3 Preheat oven to 325°F.
4 Bring cream, milk and rind to the boil in small saucepan. Beat egg yolks and sugar in small bowl with electric mixer until thick and creamy. Gradually beat hot cream mixture into egg mixture; allow bubbles to subside. Strain custard into medium jug, divide between cases.
5 Bake tarts about 25 minutes. Cool. Refrigerate tarts 2 hours.
6 Make toffee.
7 Remove tarts from pan; place on oven tray. Sprinkle custard with toffee; using blowtorch, heat until toffee caramelizes.

pastry Process flour, sugar, rind and butter until crumbly. With motor operating, add egg yolk and enough of the water to make ingredients come together. Turn dough onto floured surface, knead gently until smooth. Wrap pastry in plastic; refrigerate 30 minutes.

toffee Stir sugar and the water in medium saucepan over heat, without boiling, until sugar dissolves. Bring to the boil. Boil, uncovered, without stirring, until golden brown. Pour toffee on greased oven tray to set. Break toffee into large pieces; process until chopped finely.

prep + cook time
1 hour 10 minutes
(+ refrigeration & cooling)
makes 24

chocolate tartlets

If pastry is too dry, add 2 teaspoons of water with the egg yolk.

- 5 ounces dark semi-sweet chocolate, chopped coarsely
- ¼ cup heavy cream
- 1 tablespoon orange-flavored liqueur
- 1 egg
- 2 egg yolks
- 2 tablespoons superfine sugar

pastry
- 1⅔ cups plain (all-purpose) flour
- ⅓ cup superfine sugar
- ½ ounce cold butter, chopped coarsely
- 1 egg yolk

1 Make pastry.
2 Grease two 12-hole (2-tablespoon) deep flat-based patty pans.
3 Roll pastry between sheets of baking paper to ⅛-inch thickness; cut out 24 x 2¾-inch rounds. Press rounds into pan holes; prick bases all over with fork. Refrigerate 30 minutes.
4 Preheat oven to 400°F.
5 Bake pastry cases 10 minutes. Cool. Reduce oven to 350°F.
6 Stir chocolate, cream and liqueur in small saucepan over low heat until smooth. Cool 5 minutes.
7 Meanwhile, beat egg, egg yolks and sugar in small bowl with electric mixer until light and fluffy; fold chocolate mixture into egg mixture.
8 Divide filling into pastry cases. Bake 8 minutes; cool 10 minutes. Refrigerate 1 hour.
9 Serve tartlets dusted with a little sifted cocoa powder.

pastry Process flour, sugar and butter until coarse. Add egg yolk; process until combined. Knead pastry on floured surface until smooth. Cover; refrigerate 30 minutes.

prep + cook time
50 minutes (+ refrigeration)
makes 24

crème brûlée praline tarts

If pastry is a little too dry, add 2 teaspoons of water with the egg yolk.

1¼ cups plain (all-purpose) flour
¼ cup superfine sugar
4 ounces cold butter, chopped coarsely
1 egg yolk
1⅓ cups light cream
⅓ cup milk
1 vanilla bean
4 egg yolks
¼ cup superfine sugar, extra

praline
¼ cup superfine sugar
2 tablespoons water
2 tablespoons roasted unsalted pistachios
1 tablespoon roasted hazelnuts

1 Process flour, sugar and butter until coarse. Add egg yolk; process until combined. Knead on floured surface until smooth. Roll pastry between sheets of parchment paper until ⅛-inch thick. Refrigerate 15 minutes.
2 Grease six-hole (¾-cup) texas muffin pan. Cut six 4½-inch rounds from pastry. Press rounds into pan holes; prick bases with fork. Refrigerate 30 minutes.
3 Preheat oven to 350°F.
4 Combine cream and milk in small saucepan. Split vanilla bean in half lengthways; scrape seeds into pan (reserve pod for another use). Bring to the boil. Beat egg yolks and extra sugar in small bowl with electric mixer until thick and creamy. Gradually whisk hot cream mixture into egg mixture. Pour warm custard into pastry cases.
5 Bake tarts about 30 minutes or until set; cool 15 minutes. Refrigerate 1 hour.

6 Meanwhile, make praline.
7 Preheat grill (broiler).
8 Remove tarts from pan; place on oven tray. Sprinkle custard with praline; grill until praline caramelizes. Serve immediately.

praline Stir sugar and the water in small saucepan over heat until sugar dissolves. Boil, uncovered, without stirring, about 8 minutes or until golden. Place nuts, in single layer, on greased oven tray. Pour toffee over nuts; stand 15 minutes or until set. Break toffee into pieces; process until fine.

prep + cook time
1 hour 15 minutes (+ refrigeration, standing & cooling)
makes 6

caramel tarts

18 butternut snap cookies
12½ ounces canned sweetened
    condensed milk
2 ounces butter, chopped
    coarsely
⅓ cup firmly packed light
    brown sugar
1 tablespoon lemon juice

1 Preheat oven to 325°F. Grease two 12-hole (1½-tablespoon) shallow round-based patty pans.
2 Place one cookie each over top of 18 pan holes. Bake about 4 minutes or until cookies soften. Using the back of a teaspoon, gently press softened cookies into pan holes; cool.
3 Combine condensed milk, butter and sugar in small heavy-based saucepan; stir over heat until smooth. Bring to the boil; boil, stirring, about 10 minutes or until mixture is thick and dark caramel in color. Remove from heat; stir in juice.
4 Divide mixture among biscuit cases; refrigerate 30 minutes or until set.

prep + cook time
35 minutes (+ refrigeration)
makes 18

Little Cakes

There's something incredibly satisfying about making and decorating little cakes. They're so pretty and luscious-looking and you can be as generous with the icing or filling as you like. Most little cakes are best made on the day they are to be eaten.

mini sponge rolls

4 eggs
1¼ cups ground almonds
1 cup confectioners' sugar
⅓ cup plain (all-purpose) flour
1 ounce unsalted butter, melted
4 egg whites
1 tablespoon superfine sugar
2 tablespoons desiccated coconut
1 tablespoon granulated sugar
⅔ cup red currant jelly, warmed, strained

mock cream

½ cup superfine sugar
¼ cup water
1 tablespoon milk
¼ teaspoon gelatin
4 ounces unsalted butter, softened
1 teaspoon vanilla extract

1 Preheat oven to 425°F. Mark three 8-inch x 10-inch rectangles on three sheets baking paper. Grease three oven trays; line with parchment paper, marked-side down.
2 Beat eggs, ground almonds and sifted confectioners' sugar in small bowl with electric mixer until creamy; beat in flour. Transfer mixture to large bowl; stir in butter.
3 Beat egg whites in clean small bowl with electric mixer until soft peaks form; add superfine sugar, beat until dissolved. Fold into almond mixture, in two batches.
4 Divide mixture between trays, spread inside rectangles. Bake, one at a time, about 7 minutes.
5 Meanwhile, cut three pieces of parchment paper the same size as the base of 10-inch x 13-inch swiss roll pan; place paper on bench. Sprinkle one piece of paper with half the coconut, one with half the white sugar and the other with combined remaining coconut and white sugar. Turn each sponge onto parchment paper; peel away lining paper.

Cut crisp edges from all sides of sponges. Roll sponges from long side, using paper as guide; unroll, then cool.
6 Meanwhile, make mock cream.
7 Spread each sponge with cold jelly and mock cream, then re-roll sponges. Cover; refrigerate 30 minutes. Cut each roll into eight pieces.

mock cream Stir sugar, 2 tablespoons of the water and milk in small saucepan over low heat, without boiling, until sugar dissolves. Sprinkle gelatin over the remaining water in small jug; stir into milk mixture until gelatin dissolves. Cool. Beat butter and extract in small bowl with electric mixer until as white as possible. Gradually beat in milk mixture until light and fluffy.

prep + cook time 55 minutes (+ refrigeration & cooling)
makes 24

madeleines

2 eggs
2 tablespoons superfine sugar
2 tablespoons confectioners'
   sugar
1 teaspoon vanilla extract
¼ cup self-raising flour
¼ cup plain (all-purpose) flour
2½ ounces butter, melted
1 tablespoon hot water
2 tablespoons confectioners'
   sugar, extra

1 Preheat oven to 400°F. Grease two 12-hole (1½-tablespoon) madeleine pans with a little butter.
2 Beat eggs, superfine sugar, confectioners' sugar and extract in small bowl with electric mixer until thick and creamy.
3 Meanwhile, sift flours twice. Sift flours over egg mixture; pour combined butter and the water down side of bowl then fold ingredients together.
4 Drop rounded tablespoons of mixture into pan holes.
5 Bake madeleines about 10 minutes. Tap hot pan firmly on bench to release madeleines then turn immediately onto parchment-paper-covered wire racks to cool. Serve dusted with extra sifted confectioners' sugar.

prep + cook time 25 minutes
makes 24

carrot cakes

⅓ cup vegetable oil
½ cup firmly packed light brown sugar
1 egg
1 cup firmly packed, coarsely grated carrot
⅓ cup finely chopped walnuts
¾ cup self-raising flour
½ teaspoon mixed spice
1 tablespoon pepitas, chopped finely
1 tablespoon finely chopped dried apricots
1 tablespoon finely chopped walnuts, extra

lemon cream cheese frosting
3 ounces cream cheese, softened
1 ounce unsalted butter, softened
1 teaspoon finely grated lemon rind
1½ cups confectioners' sugar

1 Preheat oven to 350°F. Line 18 holes of two 12-hole (2-tablespoon) deep flat-based patty pans with paper cases.
2 Beat oil, sugar and egg in small bowl with electric mixer until thick and creamy. Stir in carrot and nuts, then sifted flour and spice. Divide mixture into paper cases.
3 Bake cakes about 20 minutes. Stand cakes 5 minutes before turning top-side up onto wire rack to cool.
4 Meanwhile, make lemon cream cheese frosting.
5 Spoon lemon cream cheese frosting into piping bag fitted with ¾-inch fluted tube; pipe frosting onto cakes. Sprinkle cakes with combined pepitas, apricots and extra nuts.

lemon cream cheese frosting
Beat cream cheese, butter and rind in small bowl with electric mixer until light and fluffy; gradually beat in sifted confectioners' sugar.

prep + cook time
45 minutes (+ cooling)
makes 18

black forest gateaux

It is fine to use just one 10 oz. carton of heavy cream for this recipe.

6 ounces unsalted butter, softened
1½ cups superfine sugar
6 eggs, separated
¾ cup self-raising flour
⅔ cup cocoa powder
2 tablespoons milk
½ cup blackcurrant liqueur or cherry brandy
1 cup black cherry jam
1¼ cups heavy cream, whipped
1 cup seeded drained sour cherries, halved

chocolate ganache
½ cup light cream
7 ounces dark semi-sweet chocolate, chopped coarsely

1 Preheat oven to 350°F. Grease 8-inch x 12-inch lamington pan; line with parchment paper, extending paper 2 inches over long sides.
2 Beat butter, sugar and egg yolks in small bowl with electric mixer until light and fluffy. Stir in sifted flour and cocoa and milk, in two batches.
3 Beat egg whites in clean small bowl with electric mixer until soft peaks form. Fold egg whites into cake mixture, in two batches. Spread mixture into pan.
4 Bake cake about 35 minutes. Stand cake 5 minutes before turning top-side up onto wire rack to cool.
5 Meanwhile, make chocolate ganache.
6 Trim edges from all sides of cake; cut cake into 40 squares. Split each square in half; brush each half with liqueur. Sandwich cakes with jam and cream; top with chocolate ganache and cherries.

chocolate ganache Bring cream to the boil in small saucepan. Remove from heat; pour over chocolate in small bowl, stir until smooth. Stand at room temperature until thickened slightly.

prep + cook time
1 hour 15 minutes (+ cooling)
makes 40

apple cinnamon tea loaves

3 ounces butter, softened
1 teaspoon vanilla extract
½ cup superfine sugar
1 egg
1⅓ cups self-raising flour
½ cup milk
1 medium red apple, quartered, cored, sliced thinly
½ ounce butter, melted
1 tablespoon granulated sugar
½ teaspoon ground cinnamon

spiced honey cream
⅔ cup thick cream
2 teaspoons honey
¼ teaspoon ground ginger
pinch ground cinnamon

1 Preheat oven to 350°F. Grease 8-hole (¾-cup) petite loaf pan.
2 Beat softened butter, extract and superfine sugar in small bowl with electric mixer until light and fluffy. Add egg, beat until combined. Stir in sifted flour and milk, in two batches.
3 Divide mixture into pan holes; top with apple, brush with melted butter, sprinkle with half the combined granulated sugar and cinnamon.

4 Bake loaves about 20 minutes. Sprinkle hot loaves with remaining sugar and cinnamon mixture. Stand loaves 5 minutes before turning top-side up onto wire rack to cool.
5 Meanwhile, make spiced honey cream.
6 Serve warm cakes with spiced honey cream.

spiced honey cream Combine ingredients in small bowl.

prep + cook time 35 minutes
makes 8

mini chocolate hazelnut cakes

3 ounces dark semi-sweet chocolate, chopped coarsely
¾ cup water
3 ounces butter, softened
1 cup firmly packed light brown sugar
3 eggs
¼ cup cocoa powder
¾ cup self-raising flour
⅓ cup ground hazelnuts

whipped hazelnut ganache

⅓ cup heavy cream
6 ounces milk chocolate, chopped finely
2 tablespoons hazelnut-flavored liqueur

1 Preheat oven to 350°F. Grease 12-hole (½-cup) oval friand pan.
2 Make whipped hazelnut ganache.
3 Meanwhile, combine chocolate and the water in medium saucepan; stir over low heat until smooth.
4 Beat butter and sugar in small bowl with electric mixer until light and fluffy. Add eggs, one at a time, beating until just combined between additions (mixture might separate at this stage, but will come together later); transfer mixture to medium bowl. Stir in warm chocolate mixture, sifted cocoa and flour, and ground hazelnuts. Divide mixture into pan holes.
5 Bake cakes about 20 minutes. Stand cakes 5 minutes; turn, top-sides up, onto wire rack to cool. Spread ganache over cakes.

whipped hazelnut ganache

Combine cream and chocolate in small saucepan; stir over low heat until smooth. Stir in liqueur; transfer mixture to small bowl. Cover; stand about 2 hours or until just firm. Beat ganache in small bowl with electric mixer until mixture changes to a pale brown color.

prep + cook time 1 hour (+ standing) makes 12

rhubarb and almond cakes

These days, rhubarb is available all year. Be sure to discard every bit of the vegetable's leaf and use only the thinnest stalks (the thick ones tend to be stringy).

½ cup milk
¼ cup blanched almonds, roasted
2½ ounces butter, softened
1 teaspoon vanilla extract
½ cup superfine sugar
2 eggs
1 cup self-raising flour

poached rhubarb

8 ounces trimmed rhubarb, chopped coarsely
¼ cup water
½ cup granulated sugar

1 Preheat oven to 350°F. Grease a 6-hole texas (¾-cup) muffin pan.
2 Make poached rhubarb.
3 Meanwhile, blend or process milk and nuts until smooth.
4 Beat butter, extract and sugar in small bowl with electric mixer until light and fluffy. Add eggs, one at a time, beating until just combined between additions (mixture might separate at this stage, but will come together later); transfer to large bowl. Stir in sifted flour and almond mixture. Divide mixture into pan holes.

5 Bake cakes 10 minutes. Carefully remove muffin pan from oven; divide drained rhubarb over muffins, bake further 15 minutes.
6 Stand muffins 5 minutes; turn, top-side up, onto wire rack to cool. Serve warm or cold with rhubarb syrup.

poached rhubarb Place ingredients in medium saucepan; bring to the boil. Reduce heat; simmer, uncovered, about 10 minutes or until rhubarb is just tender. Drain rhubarb over medium bowl; reserve rhubarb and syrup separately.

prep + cook time 1 hour
makes 6

passionfruit curd sponge cakes

You need four passionfruit to get the required amount of passionfruit pulp needed for this recipe.

3 eggs
½ cup superfine sugar
¾ cup self-raising flour
¾ ounce butter
¼ cup boiling water

passionfruit curd
⅓ cup passionfruit pulp
½ cup superfine sugar
2 eggs, beaten lightly
4 ounces unsalted butter, chopped coarsely

1 Make passionfruit curd.
2 Preheat oven to 350°F. Grease 12-hole (½-cup) oval friand pan with softened butter; dust lightly with flour.
3 Beat eggs in small bowl with electric mixer until thick and creamy. Gradually add sugar, beating until dissolved between additions. Transfer mixture to large bowl. Fold in sifted flour then combined butter and the boiling water. Divide mixture into pan holes.
4 Bake cakes about 12 minutes. Working quickly, loosen edges of cakes from pan using a small knife; turn immediately onto baking-paper-covered wire racks to cool.
5 Split cooled cakes in half. Spread cut-sides with curd; replace tops. Serve lightly dusted with a little sifted confectioners' sugar.

passionfruit curd Stir ingredients in medium heatproof bowl over pan of simmering water about 10 minutes or until mixture coats the back of a wooden spoon. Cover; refrigerate 3 hours.

prep + cook time 40 minutes (+ refrigeration & cooling)
makes 12

gluten-free berry cupcakes

4 ounces butter, softened
2 teaspoons finely grated lemon rind
¾ cup superfine sugar
4 eggs
2 cups ground almonds
½ cup desiccated coconut
½ cup rice flour
1 teaspoon baking soda
1 cup frozen mixed berries
1 tablespoon desiccated coconut, extra

1 Preheat oven to 350°F. Line 12-hole (⅓-cup) muffin pan with paper liners.

2 Beat butter, rind and sugar in small bowl with electric mixer until light and fluffy. Add eggs, one at a time, beating until just combined between additions (mixture will separate at this stage, but will come together later); transfer to large bowl. Stir in ground almonds, coconut, sifted flour and baking soda, then the berries. Divide mixture into paper cases.

3 Bake cakes about 25 minutes. Stand cupcakes 5 minutes; turn, top-sides up, onto wire rack to cool. Sprinkle with extra coconut.

prep + cook time 45 minutes
makes 12

ginger powder puffs with orange cream

2 eggs
⅓ cup superfine sugar
2 tablespoons cornstarch
1 tablespoon plain (all-purpose) flour
2 tablespoons self-raising flour
1 teaspoon cocoa powder
1½ teaspoons ground ginger
¼ teaspoon ground cinnamon

orange cream
⅔ cup heavy cream
2 tablespoons confectioners' sugar
1 teaspoon finely grated orange rind

1 Preheat oven to 350°F. Grease and flour two 12-hole (1½-tablespoon) shallow round-based patty pans.
2 Beat eggs and sugar in small bowl with electric mixer until thick and creamy. Fold in triple-sifted dry ingredients. Divide mixture into pan holes.
3 Bake about 8 minutes. Working quickly, loosen edges of cakes using palette knife, then turn immediately onto baking-paper-covered wire racks to cool.

4 Meanwhile, make orange cream.
5 Just before serving, sandwich puffs together with orange cream. Serve lightly dusted with a little sifted confectioners' sugar.

orange cream Beat cream and sifted confectioners' sugar in small bowl with electric mixer until firm peaks form; fold in rind.

prep + cook time 35 minutes
makes 12

jelly cakes with berry cream

It is fine to use just one 10 oz. carton of cream for this recipe.

- 4 ounces unsalted butter, softened
- ½ cup superfine sugar
- 2 teaspoons vanilla extract
- 2 eggs
- 1½ cups self-raising flour
- ⅓ cup milk
- 2 cups desiccated coconut
- 1¼ cups heavy cream, whipped
- 1 tablespoon confectioners' sugar
- 1 cup frozen mixed berries, chopped coarsely
- 25 fresh raspberries

mixed berry jelly

- 1 cup frozen mixed berries, thawed
- 1½ cups apple black currant juice
- ⅓ cup superfine sugar
- ¼ cup water
- 3 teaspoons gelatin

1 Preheat oven to 350°F. Grease 9-inch square cake pan well with butter; line base with parchment paper.
2 Beat butter, superfine sugar and half the extract in small bowl with electric mixer until light and fluffy. Beat in eggs, one at a time. Stir in sifted flour and milk, in two batches. Spread mixture into pan.
3 Bake cake about 25 minutes. Stand cake 5 minutes before turning top-side up onto wire rack to cool.
4 Meanwhile, make mixed berry jelly.
5 Trim edges from all sides of cake; cut cake into 25 squares. Dip each square into jelly then roll in coconut. Place on tray, cover; refrigerate 30 minutes.
6 Beat cream, confectioners' sugar and remaining extract in small bowl with electric mixer until soft peaks form; fold in berries. Split each jelly cake in half; sandwich with berry cream. Top each jelly cake with a fresh raspberry.

mixed berry jelly Blend or process berries until smooth. Stir juice, sugar and berry puree in medium saucepan over medium heat until sugar dissolves. Strain mixture through fine sieve; discard solids. Place the water in small heatproof jug; sprinkle over gelatin. Stand jug in small saucepan of simmering water, stirring, until gelatin dissolves. Stir gelatin mixture into berry mixture. Pour into shallow dish; refrigerate, stirring occasionally, until set to the consistency of unbeaten egg white.

prep + cook time
1 hour 10 minutes (+ refrigeration)
makes 25

Big Cakes

These are the star attraction at any afternoon tea. People nibble sandwiches and eat a tart or two but all the time they're waiting for you to cut the cake. A teatime cake is your opportunity to make something truly extravagant and memorable.

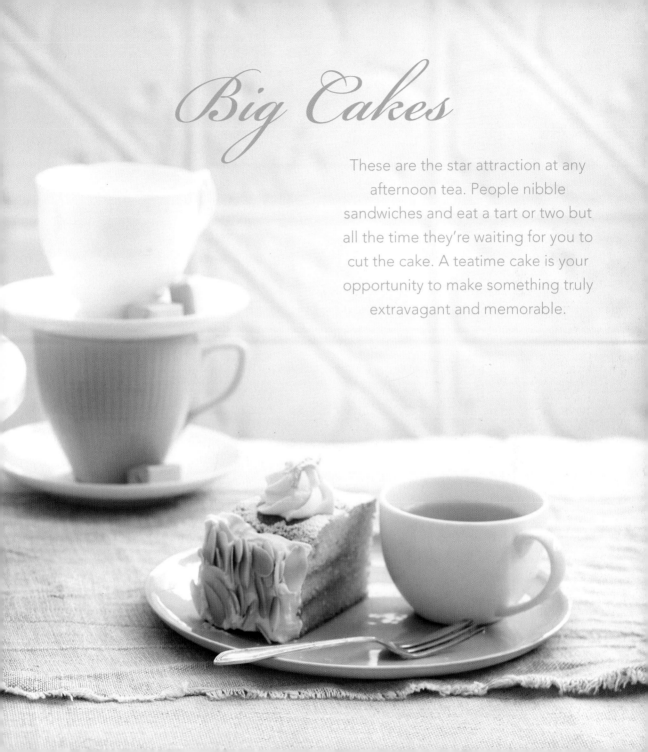

pink velvet cake

It is fine to use just one 10 oz. carton of heavy cream for this recipe.

4 ounces butter, softened
1 teaspoon vanilla extract
1½ cups superfine sugar
2 eggs
1½ cups plain (all-purpose) flour
2 tablespoons cornstarch
2 tablespoons cocoa powder
1 cup buttermilk
1 tablespoon rose pink food coloring
1 teaspoon white vinegar
1 teaspoon baking soda
1 cup flaked coconut

mascarpone frosting
8 ounces cream cheese, softened
8 ounces mascarpone cheese
1 cup confectioners' sugar
1 teaspoon vanilla extract
1¼ cups heavy cream

1 Preheat oven to 350°F. Grease two deep 9-inch round cake pans; line bases and sides with parchment paper.
2 Beat butter, extract, sugar and eggs in small bowl with electric mixer until light and fluffy. Transfer mixture to large bowl; stir in sifted flours and cocoa and combined buttermilk and food coloring, in two batches.
3 Combine vinegar and baking soda in a cup; allow to fizz then fold into cake mixture. Divide mixture between pans.
4 Bake cakes about 25 minutes. Stand cakes 10 minutes before turning top-side up onto wire racks to cool. Enclose cakes in plastic wrap; freeze 40 minutes.
5 Meanwhile, make mascarpone frosting.
6 Split cold cakes in half. Place one layer on serving plate, cut-side up; spread with ⅔ cup frosting. Repeat layering, finishing with remaining frosting spread over top and side of cake; press coconut onto side of cake.

mascarpone frosting Beat cream cheese, mascarpone, sugar and extract in small bowl with electric mixer until smooth. Beat in cream.

prep + cook time
1 hour (+ cooling & freezing)
serves 12

orange almond victoria sponge

It is fine to use just one 10 oz. carton of heavy cream for this recipe.

6 ounces unsalted butter, softened
1 teaspoon vanilla extract
¾ cup superfine sugar
3 eggs
¼ cup milk
1½ cups self-raising flour
1 cup orange marmalade, warmed
1¼ cups heavy cream
2 tablespoons confectioners' sugar
½ cup flaked almonds, roasted

1 Preheat oven to 350°F. Grease deep 8-inch ring pan well with butter.
2 Beat butter, extract, and superfine sugar in small bowl with electric mixer until light and fluffy. Beat in eggs, one at a time. Stir in milk and sifted flour, in two batches. Spread mixture into pan.
3 Bake sponge about 30 minutes. Turn sponge immediately onto parchment-paper-covered wire rack, turn top-side up to cool.
4 Meanwhile, strain marmalade through fine sieve; reserve syrup and rind separately.
5 Beat cream and half the confectioners' sugar in small bowl with electric mixer until soft peaks form.

6 Split sponge into three layers. Place one layer onto serving plate, cut-side up; spread with half of the marmalade syrup. Top with another layer of sponge and remaining syrup; top with remaining layer of sponge. Cut sponge into twelve pieces, keeping cake in ring shape.
7 Spread two-thirds of the cream around side of sponge; press almonds into cream. Spoon remaining cream into piping bag fitted with ½-inch fluted tube. Pipe rosettes on top of cake; top with some of the reserved rind. Serve sponge dusted with remaining confectioners' sugar.

prep + cook time
55 minutes (+ cooling)
serves 12

chocolate and pecan torte

If you can't find ground pecans, simply blend or process 4½ ounces of roasted pecans until they are finely ground. Be sure to use the pulse button, however, because you want to achieve a flour-like texture, not a paste.

6½ ounces dark semi-sweet chocolate, chopped coarsely
4½ ounces butter, chopped coarsely
  5 eggs, separated
  ¾ cup superfine sugar
1½ cups ground pecans

ganache
  ½ cup pouring cream
6½ ounces dark semi-sweet chocolate, chopped coarsely

1 Preheat oven to 350°F. Grease deep 9-inch round cake pan; line base and side with baking paper.
2 Stir chocolate and butter in small saucepan over low heat until smooth; cool 10 minutes.
3 Beat egg yolks and sugar in small bowl with electric mixer until thick and creamy. Transfer to large bowl; fold in chocolate mixture and ground pecans.
4 Beat egg whites in small bowl with electric mixer until soft peaks form; fold into chocolate mixture, in two batches. Pour mixture into pan.
5 Bake cake about 55 minutes. Stand cake 15 minutes; turn, top-side up, onto parchment-paper-covered wire rack to cool.

6 Meanwhile, make ganache.
7 Pour ganache over cake; refrigerate cake 30 minutes before serving.

ganache Bring cream to the boil in small saucepan. Remove from heat; add chocolate, stir until smooth.

prep + cook time
1 hour 20 minutes
(+ standing & refrigeration)
serves 8

raspberry cream sponge

Use a serrated or electric knife to split and cut the sponge.

 4 eggs
¾ cup superfine sugar
⅔ cup wheaten cornflour
¼ cup custard powder
 1 teaspoon cream of tartar
½ teaspoon baking soda
¾ cup raspberry jam
1½ cups heavy cream, whipped

raspberry glacé icing
1½ ounces fresh raspberries
 2 cups confectioners' sugar
½ ounce butter, softened
 2 teaspoons hot water, approximately

1 Preheat oven to 350°F. Grease deep 9-inch square cake pan with butter.
2 Beat eggs and sugar in small bowl with electric mixer about 10 minutes or until thick and creamy and sugar has dissolved; transfer to large bowl.
3 Sift dry ingredients twice, then sift over egg mixture; fold dry ingredients into egg mixture. Spread mixture into pan.
4 Bake sponge about 25 minutes. Turn sponge immediately onto parchment-paper-covered wire rack, then turn top-side up to cool.
5 Meanwhile, make raspberry glacé icing.
6 Split sponge in half. Sandwich with jam and cream. Spread sponge with icing, sprinkle with fresh rose petals.

raspberry glacé icing Push raspberries through fine sieve into small heatproof bowl; discard solids. Sift confectioners' sugar into same bowl; stir in butter and enough of the water to make a thick paste. Place bowl over small saucepan of simmering water; stir until icing is spreadable.

prep + cook time
50 minutes (+ cooling)
serves 16

pistachio buttercake
with orange honey syrup

Unless stated otherwise, use roasted unsalted nuts when making a cake. Buy the freshest nuts you can: they should taste slightly sweet.

2 cups roasted unsalted pistachios, chopped coarsely
6 ounces butter, softened
1 tablespoon finely grated orange rind
¾ cup superfine sugar
3 eggs
¼ cup buttermilk
1½ cups self-raising flour
¾ cup plain (all-purpose) flour

orange honey syrup
1 cup superfine sugar
1 cup water
1 tablespoon honey
1 cinnamon stick
1 teaspoon cardamom seeds
3 star anise
3 strips orange rind

1 Make orange honey syrup; cool.
2 Preheat oven to 350°F. Grease 9-inch square slab cake pan; line base and sides with parchment paper, extending paper 1 inch over sides. Sprinkle nuts over base of pan.
3 Beat butter, rind and sugar in small bowl with electric mixer until light and fluffy. Add eggs, one at a time, beating until just combined between additions; transfer mixture to large bowl. Stir in combined buttermilk and ⅓ cup of the orange honey syrup, and sifted flours, in two batches. Spread mixture into pan.
4 Bake cake about 40 minutes. Stand cake 5 minutes; turn, top-side up, onto parchment-paper-covered wire rack. Brush surface of hot cake with half of the remaining heated syrup.
5 Cut cake into squares, serve warm, drizzled with remaining heated syrup.

orange honey syrup Stir ingredients in small saucepan over low heat, without boiling, until sugar dissolves; bring to the boil. Remove from heat; cool 15 minutes then strain.

prep + cook time
1 hour 10 minutes
serves 16

lime and poppy seed syrup cake

Before grating the lime, make sure it is at room temperature and roll it, pressing down hard with your hand, on the kitchen bench. This will help extract as much juice as possible from the fruit. You can substitute the same weight of other citrus fruit – lemons, mandarins, oranges, blood oranges, etc. – for the limes if you wish.

¼ cup poppy seeds
½ cup milk
8 ounces butter, softened
1 tablespoon finely grated lime rind
1¼ cups superfine sugar
4 eggs
2¼ cups self-raising flour
¾ cup plain (all-purpose) flour
1 cup sour cream

lime syrup
½ cup lime juice
1 cup water
1 cup superfine sugar

1 Preheat oven to 350°F. Grease base and sides of deep 9-inch square cake pan.
2 Combine poppy seeds and milk in small jug; soak 10 minutes.
3 Beat butter, rind and sugar in small bowl with electric mixer until light and fluffy. Add eggs, one at a time, beating until combined between additions; transfer mixture to large bowl. Stir in sifted flours, sour cream and poppy seed mixture, in two batches. Spread mixture into pan.
4 Bake cake about 1 hour.
5 Meanwhile, make lime syrup.
6 Stand cake 5 minutes, turn onto wire rack over tray. Pour hot lime syrup over hot cake.

lime syrup Stir ingredients in small saucepan over heat, without boiling, until sugar dissolves. Simmer, uncovered, without stirring, 5 minutes.

prep + cook time
1 hour 20 minutes
serves 16

tiramisu roulade

Use any coffee-flavored liqueur you prefer in the mascarpone cream filling – you could also use chocolate, almond or hazelnut liqueur. This roulade uses all-purpose rather than self-raising flour; its rising is thanks to the air incorporated into the eggs.

¼ cup water
2 tablespoons coffee-flavored liqueur
2 tablespoons superfine sugar
1 tablespoon instant coffee granules
1 tablespoon boiling water
3 eggs
½ cup superfine sugar, extra
½ cup plain (all-purpose) flour
2 tablespoons flaked almonds
2 teaspoons superfine sugar, extra

coffee liqueur cream
1 cup mascarpone cheese
½ cup heavy)cream
2 tablespoons coffee-flavored liqueur

1 Preheat oven to 425°F. Grease 10-inch x 16-inch swiss roll pan; line base and two long sides with baking paper, extending paper 2 inches over long sides.
2 Bring the water, liqueur and sugar to the boil in small saucepan. Reduce heat; simmer, uncovered, without stirring, about 5 minutes or until syrup thickens slightly. Remove from heat, stir in half the coffee; reserve syrup.
3 Dissolve remaining coffee in the boiling water.
4 Beat eggs and extra sugar in small bowl with electric mixer about 5 minutes or until sugar is dissolved and mixture is thick; transfer to large bowl, fold in dissolved coffee.
5 Sift flour twice onto paper. Sift flour over egg mixture then fold gently into mixture. Spread sponge mixture into pan; sprinkle with nuts.
6 Bake sponge about 15 minutes.

7 Meanwhile, place a piece of parchment paper cut the same size as swiss roll pan on bench; sprinkle evenly with a little more superfine sugar. Turn sponge onto sugared paper; peel away lining paper. Use serrated knife to cut crisp edges from all sides of sponge. Roll sponge from long side, using paper as guide; cool.
8 Meanwhile, make coffee liqueur cream.
9 Unroll sponge, brush with reserved syrup. Spread cream over sponge then re-roll sponge. Cover with plastic wrap; refrigerate 30 minutes before serving.

coffee liqueur cream Beat ingredients in small bowl with electric mixer until firm peaks form.

prep + cook time
55 minutes (+ refrigeration)
serves 8

berry cream roulade

3 eggs
½ cup superfine sugar
½ cup wheaten cornflour
1 tablespoon custard powder
1 teaspoon cream of tartar
½ teaspoon baking soda
1 tablespoon superfine sugar, extra
1 tablespoon confectioners' sugar

berry cream

¾ cup heavy cream
1 teaspoon vanilla extract
1 tablespoon confectioners' sugar
1 cup frozen blackberries, chopped coarsely

1 Preheat oven to 350°F. Grease 10-inch x 12-inch swiss roll pan; line base and two long sides with parchment paper, extending paper 2 inches over long sides.
2 Beat eggs and superfine sugar in small bowl with electric mixer about 5 minutes or until sugar is dissolved and mixture is thick and creamy; transfer to large bowl.
3 Sift cornflour, custard powder, cream of tartar and baking soda together twice onto paper then sift over egg mixture; gently fold dry ingredients into egg mixture. Spread sponge mixture into pan.
4 Bake sponge about 12 minutes.
5 Meanwhile, place a piece of parchment paper cut the same size as swiss roll pan on bench; sprinkle evenly with extra superfine sugar. Turn sponge onto sugared paper; peel away lining paper. Use serrated knife to cut away crisp edges from all sides of sponge. Roll sponge from long side, using paper as a guide; cover with a tea towel, then cool.

6 Meanwhile, make berry cream.
7 Unroll sponge, spread cream over sponge then re-roll sponge. Dust with sifted confectioners' sugar.

berry cream Beat cream, extract and icing sugar in small bowl with electric mixer until soft peaks form; fold in thawed berries.

prep + cook time 30 minutes
serves 8

lemon and lime white chocolate mud cake

Grate the citrus rind called for here then save the fruit to extract the juice for another use. Without this protective "skin," the fruit will become dry and hard, so they should be juiced, say for a salsa or salad dressing, within a day or two.

8 ounces butter, chopped
2 teaspoons each finely grated lemon rind and lime rind
5½ ounces white chocolate, chopped coarsely
1½ cups superfine sugar
¾ cup milk
1½ cups plain (all-purpose) flour
½ cup self-raising flour
2 eggs, beaten lightly

coconut ganache
11½ ounces white chocolate, chopped finely
1 teaspoon each finely grated lemon rind and lime rind
½ cup coconut cream

1 Preheat oven to 340°F. Grease deep 8-inch round cake pan; line base with parchment paper.
2 Stir butter, rinds, chocolate, sugar and milk in medium saucepan over low heat until smooth. Transfer mixture to large bowl; cool 15 minutes.
3 Stir in sifted flours and egg; pour mixture into pan.
4 Bake about 1 hour 40 minutes; cool cake in pan.
5 Meanwhile, make coconut ganache.
6 Turn cake, top-side up, onto serving plate; spread ganache over cake.

coconut ganache Combine chocolate and rinds in medium bowl. Bring coconut cream to the boil in small saucepan; pour over chocolate mixture, stir until smooth. Cover bowl; refrigerate, stirring occasionally, about 30 minutes or until ganache is spreadable.

prep + cook time
2 hours 20 minutes
(+ cooling & refrigeration)
serves 10

chocolate banana cake

You will need about 2 large overripe bananas for this recipe. It is very important that the bananas you use are overripe; less-ripe ones won't mash easily and can cause the cake to be too heavy.

- ⅔ cup milk
- 2 teaspoons lemon juice
- 4½ ounces butter, softened
- 1 cup superfine sugar
- 2 eggs
- 2 cups self-raising flour
- ½ teaspoon baking soda
- 1 cup mashed banana
- 3 ounces dark semi-sweet chocolate, grated finely

creamy choc frosting
- 6½ ounces dark semi-sweet chocolate, chopped coarsely
- 1 cup confectioners' sugar
- ½ cup sour cream

1 Preheat oven to 340°F. Grease deep 9-inch round cake pan; line base with parchment paper.
2 Combine milk and juice in small jug; stand 10 minutes.
3 Meanwhile, beat butter and sugar in small bowl with electric mixer until light and fluffy. Beat in eggs, one at a time; transfer mixture to large bowl. Stir in sifted flour and baking soda, banana, milk mixture and chocolate.
4 Spread mixture into pan; bake about 1 hour 10 minutes. Stand cake 5 minutes before turning, top-side up, onto wire rack to cool.
5 Meanwhile, make creamy choc frosting. Spread cold cake with frosting.

creamy choc frosting Melt chocolate in medium heatproof bowl over medium saucepan of simmering water; gradually stir in sifted confectioners' sugar and sour cream.

prep + cook time
1 hour 30 minutes
serves 10

brown sugar sponge

It is fine to use just one 10 oz. carton of cream for this recipe. Filled sponge is best eaten the day it is made. Unfilled sponge can be frozen for up to 2 months.

- 4 eggs
- ¾ cup firmly packed dark brown sugar
- 1 cup wheaten cornflour
- 1 teaspoon cream of tartar
- ½ teaspoon baking soda
- 1¼ cups heavy cream

praline

- ⅓ cup granulated sugar
- ¼ cup water
- ½ teaspoon malt vinegar
- ⅓ cup roasted hazelnuts

1 Preheat oven to 350°F. Grease two deep 9-inch round cake pans.

2 Beat eggs and brown sugar in small bowl with electric mixer about 10 minutes or until thick and creamy; transfer to large bowl.

3 Sift cornflour, cream of tartar and baking soda twice onto paper then sift over egg mixture; gently fold dry ingredients into egg mixture. Divide mixture between pans.

4 Bake cakes about 18 minutes. Turn immediately onto parchment-paper-covered wire racks to cool.

5 Meanwhile, make praline.

6 Beat cream in small bowl with electric mixer until firm peaks form; fold in praline. Place one sponge on serving plate; spread with half the cream mixture. Top with remaining sponge; spread with remaining cream mixture.

praline Stir sugar, the water and vinegar in small saucepan over heat, without boiling, until sugar dissolves; bring to the boil. Reduce heat; simmer, uncovered, without stirring, about 10 minutes or until syrup is golden brown. Add hazelnuts; pour praline mixture onto parchment-paper-lined tray. Cool about 15 minutes or until set. Break praline into pieces then blend or process until mixture is as fine (or as coarse) as desired.

prep + cook time
50 minutes (+ cooling)
serves 8

fresh ginger cake with golden ginger cream

It is fine to use just one 10 oz. carton of cream in the golden ginger cream recipe.

8 ounces butter, chopped
½ cup firmly packed light brown sugar
⅔ cup golden syrup or treacle
4¾-inch piece fresh ginger, grated finely
1 cup plain (all-purpose) flour
1 cup self-raising flour
½ teaspoon baking soda
2 eggs, beaten lightly
¾ cup heavy cream

golden ginger cream
1¼ cups heavy cream
2 tablespoons golden syrup or treacle
2 teaspoons ground ginger

1 Preheat oven to 350°F. Grease deep 9-inch round cake pan.
2 Melt butter in medium saucepan, add sugar, syrup and ginger; stir over low heat until sugar dissolves.
3 Whisk in combined sifted flours and parchment soda then egg and cream. Pour mixture into pan.
4 Bake cake about 50 minutes. Stand cake 10 minutes; turn, top-side up, onto wire rack to cool.
5 Meanwhile, make golden ginger cream.
6 Serve cake with cream.

golden ginger cream Beat ingredients in small bowl with electric mixer until soft peaks form.

prep + cook time
1 hour 15 minutes
serves 10

lemon cake

Grate the lemon for the frosting before you extract the juice for the cake mixture. Frosted cake will keep in an airtight container, in the fridge, for up to 3 days.

- 4 ounces butter, softened
- 2 teaspoons finely grated lemon rind
- 1¼ cups superfine sugar
- 3 eggs
- 1½ cups self-raising flour
- ½ cup milk
- ¼ cup lemon juice

lemon mascarpone frosting
- 1 cup heavy cream
- ½ cup confectioners' sugar
- 2 teaspoons finely grated lemon rind
- ⅔ cup mascarpone cheese

1 Preheat oven to 350°F. Grease deep 8-inch round cake pan; line base with parchment paper.
2 Make lemon mascarpone frosting. Refrigerate, covered, until required.
3 Beat butter, rind and sugar in small bowl with electric mixer until light and fluffy. Beat in eggs, one at a time (mixture might separate at this stage, but will come together later); transfer mixture to large bowl. Stir in sifted flour, milk and juice, in two batches. Pour mixture into pan.
4 Bake cake about 50 minutes. Stand cake in pan 5 minutes before turning, top-side up, onto wire rack to cool.
5 Split cold cake into three layers, place one layer onto serving plate, cut-side up; spread with one-third of the frosting. Repeat layering process, finishing with frosting.

lemon mascarpone frosting
Beat cream, sifted confectioners' sugar and rind in small bowl with electric mixer until soft peaks form. Fold cream mixture into mascarpone.

prep + cook time
1 hour 20 minutes
serves 8

upside-down toffee date and banana cake

You will need 1 large overripe banana for the amount of mashed banana. It is important that the banana you use is overripe; less-ripe ones won't mash easily and can cause the cake to be too heavy. We prefer to use an underproof rum in baking. It is fine to use just one 10 oz. carton of cream for this recipe.

1½ cups superfine sugar
1½ cups water
3 star anise
2 medium bananas, sliced thinly
1 cup seeded dried dates
¾ cup water, extra
½ cup dark rum
1 teaspoon baking soda
2 ounces butter, chopped
½ cup firmly packed light brown sugar
2 eggs
2 teaspoons mixed spice
1 cup self-raising flour
½ cup mashed banana
1¼ cups heavy cream

1 Preheat oven to 350°F. Grease deep 9-inch round cake pan; line base with parchment paper.
2 Stir superfine sugar, the water and star anise in medium saucepan over low heat, without boiling, until sugar dissolves. Bring to a boil; boil syrup, uncovered, without stirring, about 5 minutes or until thickened slightly. Strain ½ cup of the syrup into small heatproof jug; reserve to flavor cream. Discard star-anise.
3 To make toffee, continue boiling remaining syrup, uncovered, without stirring, about 10 minutes or until toffee is golden brown. Pour hot toffee into cake pan; top with sliced banana.

4 Place dates, the extra water and rum in small saucepan; bring to the boil then remove from heat. Stir in baking soda; stand 5 minutes. Blend or process date mixture with butter and brown sugar until almost smooth. Add eggs, spice and flour; blend or process until just combined. Stir in mashed banana. Pour mixture into pan.
5 Bake cake about 40 minutes. Turn cake, in pan, onto serving plate; stand 2 minutes. Remove pan then baking paper.
6 To make star anise cream, beat cream in small bowl with electric mixer until firm peaks form. Stir in reserved syrup.
7 Serve cake warm or at room temperature with star anise cream.

prep + cook time
1 hour 30 minutes
serves 8

spices of the orient teacake

The secret to a successful teacake lies in the beating of the sugar, egg and butter – the mixture must be very light in color and full of air.

  2 ounces butter, softened
  1 teaspoon vanilla extract
  ½ cup superfine sugar
  1 egg
  1 cup self-raising flour
  ⅓ cup milk
  ¾ ounce butter, melted, extra

spiced nuts
  2 tablespoons shelled pistachios, chopped finely
  2 tablespoons blanched almonds, chopped finely
  2 tablespoons pine nuts, chopped finely
  ¼ cup confectioners' sugar
  1 teaspoon ground cinnamon
  ½ teaspoon each ground allspice and ground cardamom

1 Preheat oven to 350°F. Grease 8-inch round cake pan.
2 Beat butter, extract, sugar and egg in small bowl with electric mixer until light and fluffy. Stir in sifted flour and milk. Spread mixture into pan.
3 Bake cake about 25 minutes. Stand cake 5 minutes; turn, top-side up, onto wire rack to cool.
4 Meanwhile, make spiced nuts.
5 Brush cooled cake with extra butter; sprinkle with spiced nuts. Serve warm.

spiced nuts Place nuts in strainer; rinse under cold water. Combine wet nuts in large bowl with confectioners' sugar and spices; spread mixture onto oven tray, roast in oven about 10 minutes or until nuts are dry.

prep + cook time 45 minutes
serves 10

boiled whiskey fruit cake

This rich fruit cake will keep indefinitely if stored in an airtight container in a clean cool, dark place, or in the fridge or freezer.

1½ cups raisins
1½ cups seeded dried dates
1½ cups seeded prunes
1½ cups golden raisins
⅓ cup red glacé cherries, quartered
⅓ cup mixed peel
2 tablespoons superfine sugar
1 ounce butter
½ cup whiskey
8 ounces butter, chopped, extra
1 cup firmly packed dark brown sugar
½ teaspoon baking soda
½ cup slivered almonds
2 cups plain (all-purpose) flour
2 teaspoons mixed spice
5 eggs
¼ cup whiskey, extra

1 Chop raisins, dates and prunes the same size as the golden raisins (this will help make the finished cake cut better); combine in a large bowl with golden raisins, cherries and peel.
2 Place superfine sugar in large heavy-based saucepan over medium heat; turn pan occasionally until sugar is melted. Add butter and whiskey; stir over low heat until smooth.
3 Add extra butter, brown sugar and fruit to pan. Stir over heat until butter melts; bring to the boil. Remove from heat; stir in baking soda. Transfer to large bowl, cover; stand overnight at room temperature.
4 Preheat oven to 300°F. Grease deep 8-inch square cake pan; line base and sides with two layers of brown paper then parchment paper, extending paper 2 inches over sides.

5 Add nuts, sifted flour and spice, and eggs to fruit mixture; stir until well combined.
6 Spoon mixture into corners of pan then spread remaining mixture into pan. Drop pan from a height of about 6 inches onto bench to settle mixture into pan and to break any large air bubbles; level surface of cake with wet spatula.
7 Bake cake about 3 hours. Brush hot cake with extra whiskey. Cover hot cake tightly with foil; cool in pan.

prep + cook time
3 hours 35 minutes (+ standing)
serves 20

almond carrot cake

Store iced cake in an airtight container, in the fridge, for up to 4 days.

- 5 eggs, separated
- 1 teaspoon finely grated lemon rind
- 1¼ cups superfine sugar
- 2 cups coarsely grated carrot
- 2 cups ground almonds
- ½ cup self-raising flour
- 2 tablespoons roasted slivered almonds

cream cheese frosting

- 3 ounces cream cheese, softened
- 2½ ounces butter, softened
- ½ cup confectioners' sugar
- 1 teaspoon lemon juice

1 Preheat oven to 350°F. Grease deep 8-inch square cake pan; line base with parchment paper.
2 Beat egg yolks, rind and sugar in small bowl with electric mixer until thick and creamy; transfer to large bowl. Stir in carrot, ground almonds and sifted flour.
3 Beat egg whites in small bowl with electric mixer until soft peaks form; fold into carrot mixture, in two batches. Pour mixture into pan.
4 Bake cake about 1¼ hours. Stand cake 5 minutes before turning, top-side up, onto wire rack to cool.
5 Meanwhile, make cream cheese frosting.
6 Spread cold cake with cream cheese frosting; sprinkle with slivered almonds.

cream cheese frosting Beat cream cheese and butter in small bowl with electric mixer until light and fluffy; gradually beat in sifted confectioners' sugar and juice.

prep + cook time
1 hour 35 minutes
serves 10

muscat prune shortcake

It is fine to use just one 10 oz. carton of cream for this recipe. A fortified wine, like sherry and port, muscat is the result of grapes left to ripen well beyond normal harvesting time, resulting in a concentrated dark, toffee-colored wine with a rich yet mellow flavor.

6½ ounces butter, softened
1 teaspoon finely grated lemon rind
⅓ cup superfine sugar
¼ cup rice flour
¾ cup self-raising flour
¾ cup plain (all-purpose) flour
1¼ cups heavy cream
1 tablespoon superfine sugar, extra

muscat prunes
1 cup seeded prunes, chopped coarsely
1 cup muscat

1 Preheat oven to 350°F. Grease three 8-inch round sandwich pans.
2 Beat butter, rind and sugar in medium bowl with electric mixer until light and fluffy. Fold in sifted flours, in two batches. Press mixture evenly into pans.
3 Bake shortcakes about 20 minutes. Stand shortcakes in pans; cool to room temperature.
4 Meanwhile, make muscat prunes.
5 Beat cream in small bowl with electric mixer until firm peaks form. Place one shortcake into deep 8-inch round cake pan or 8-inch springform tin; spread with half the prune mixture then half the whipped cream. Top with another shortcake; spread with remaining prune mixture then remaining whipped cream. Top with remaining shortcake, cover; refrigerate overnight.
6 Remove shortcake from pan; serve sprinkled with extra sugar.

muscat prunes Stir prunes and muscat in small saucepan over heat, without boiling, until prunes soften. Cool to room temperature.

prep + cook time 55 minutes (+ cooling & refrigeration) serves 12

chocolate mud cake with chili cherries

8 ounces butter, chopped
6½ ounces dark semi-sweet chocolate, chopped coarsely
2 cups superfine sugar
1 cup milk
1 teaspoon vanilla extract
⅓ cup bourbon
1½ cups plain (all-purpose) flour
¼ cup self-raising flour
¼ cup cocoa powder
2 eggs

chili cherries
2 cups water
¾ cup superfine sugar
1 fresh small red thai (serrano) chili, halved lengthways
1 star anise
6 whole black peppercorns
4-inch piece orange rind
9½ ounces frozen cherries

dark chocolate ganache
⅓ cup pouring cream
6½ ounces dark semi-sweet chocolate, chopped coarsely

1 Preheat oven to 340°F. Grease deep 9-inch round cake pan; line base with parchment paper.
2 Combine butter, chocolate, sugar, milk, extract and bourbon in medium saucepan; stir over low heat until smooth. Transfer to large bowl; cool 15 minutes. Whisk in sifted flours and cocoa, then eggs. Pour mixture into pan.
3 Bake cake about 1½ hours.
4 Meanwhile, make chili cherries.
5 Stand cake in pan 5 minutes; turn, top-side up, onto wire rack to cool.
6 Meanwhile, make dark chocolate ganache.
7 Spread ganache over top and side of cake; serve with chili cherries.

chili cherries Stir the water, sugar, chili, star anise, peppercorns and rind in medium saucepan over low heat, without boiling, until sugar dissolves. Bring to the boil; boil 2 minutes. Add cherries; simmer 5 minutes or until cherries are just tender. Cool cherries in syrup. Remove cherries from pan; bring syrup to the boil. Boil 10 minutes or until syrup thickens slightly; cool. Return cherries to pan.

dark chocolate ganache Bring cream to the boil in small saucepan. Remove from heat; add chocolate, stir until smooth.

prep + cook time
1 hour 55 minutes (+ cooling)
serves 10

almond honey spice cake

4 ounces butter, softened
⅓ cup superfine sugar
2 tablespoons honey
1 teaspoon each ground
ginger and ground allspice
2 eggs
1½ cups ground almonds
½ cup semolina
1 teaspoon baking powder
¼ cup milk

spiced syrup

1 cup superfine sugar
1 cup water
8 cardamom pods, bruised
2 cinnamon sticks

honey orange cream

¾ cup heavy cream
1 tablespoon honey
2 tablespoons finely grated
orange rind

1 Preheat oven to 350°F. Grease deep 8-inch round cake pan; line base and side with parchment paper.
2 Beat butter, sugar, honey and spices in small bowl with electric mixer until light and fluffy. Beat in eggs, one at a time, until just combined between additions; transfer mixture to medium bowl. Fold in ground almonds, semolina, baking powder and milk. Spread mixture into pan.
3 Bake cake about 40 minutes. Stand cake 5 minutes.
4 Meanwhile, make spiced syrup.
5 Pour strained hot syrup over hot cake in pan; cool cake in pan to room temperature. Turn cake, in pan, upside-down onto serving plate; refrigerate 3 hours or overnight.
6 Remove cake from refrigerator. Make honey orange cream.
7 Remove cake from pan; serve cake at room temperature with honey orange cream.

spiced syrup Stir ingredients in small saucepan over heat, without boiling, until sugar dissolves; bring to the boil. Boil, uncovered, without stirring, about 5 minutes or until syrup thickens slightly.

honey orange cream Beat cream, honey and rind in small bowl with electric mixer until soft peaks form.

prep + cook time
1 hour (+ cooling, refrigeration & standing) serves 10

whipped cream cake with caramel icing

In this recipe, cream replaces milk and butter, resulting in a cake that's firm like a buttercake – even though it's made like a sponge. It is fine to use two 10 oz. (or one 20 oz.) cartons of cream for this recipe.

2⅔ cups heavy cream
 3 eggs
 1 teaspoon vanilla extract
1¼ cups firmly packed light brown sugar
 2 cups self-raising flour

caramel icing
 2 ounces butter
 ½ cup firmly packed light brown sugar
 2 tablespoons milk
 ½ cup confectioners' sugar

1 Preheat oven to 350°F. Grease deep 9-inch round cake pan; line base with parchment paper.
2 Beat half the cream in small bowl with electric mixer until soft peaks form.
3 Beat eggs and extract in small bowl with electric mixer until thick and creamy; gradually add sugar, beating until dissolved between additions. Transfer mixture to large bowl. Fold in a quarter of the whipped cream then sifted flour, then remaining whipped cream. Spread mixture into pan.
4 Bake cake about 50 minutes. Stand cake in pan 5 minutes; turn, top-side up, onto wire rack to cool.

5 Meanwhile, beat remaining cream in small bowl with electric mixer until firm peaks form.
6 Make caramel icing.
7 Split cold cake in half; sandwich layers with cream. Spread cake with caramel icing.

caramel icing Melt butter in small saucepan, add brown sugar and milk; bring to the boil. Reduce heat immediately; simmer 2 minutes. Cool to room temperature. Stir in icing sugar until smooth.

prep + cook time
1 hour 10 minutes
serves 10

quince and blackberry crumble cake

6 ounces unsalted butter, softened
¾ cup superfine sugar
2 eggs
2¼ cups self-raising flour
¾ cup milk
2 cups frozen blackberries
2 teaspoons cornstarch

poached quince

3 cups water
¾ cup superfine sugar
1 cinnamon stick
1 tablespoon lemon juice
3 medium quinces, each cut into 8 wedges

cinnamon crumble

¾ cup plain (all-purpose) flour
2 tablespoons superfine sugar
½ cup firmly packed light brown sugar
3 ounces cold unsalted butter, chopped
1 teaspoon ground cinnamon

1 Make poached quince.
2 Preheat oven to 350°F. Grease deep 9-inch square cake pan; line base and sides with baking paper.
3 Beat butter and sugar in small bowl with electric mixer until light and fluffy. Add eggs, one at a time, beating between additions until just combined; transfer to large bowl. Stir in sifted flour and milk, in two batches. Spread mixture into pan.
4 Bake cake 25 minutes.
5 Meanwhile, make cinnamon crumble.
6 Remove cake from oven. Working quickly, toss frozen blackberries in cornstarch to coat. Top cake with drained quince then blackberries; sprinkle crumble over fruit. Return to oven; bake 20 minutes.
7 Stand cake in pan 5 minutes; turn, top-side up, onto wire rack. Serve cake warm or cold with reserved quince syrup.

poached quince Stir the water, sugar, cinnamon stick and juice in medium saucepan over low heat until sugar dissolves. Add quince; bring to the boil. Reduce heat; simmer, covered, about 1½ hours or until quince is tender and rosy in color. Cool quince in syrup to room temperature; strain quince over medium bowl. Reserve quince and syrup separately.

cinnamon crumble Blend or process ingredients, pulsing until ingredients just come together.

prep + cook time
2 hours 45 minutes (+ cooling)
serves 16

Cookies

Cookies are an essential and very popular part of an afternoon tea. And their great advantage is that most of them can be made in advance (fill or ice them on the day of the tea party) which leaves you time to spend on the cake and sandwiches. Once cookies are iced or filled they go soft very quickly.

greek almond crescents

Crescents will keep in an airtight container for up to a week.

8 ounces butter, softened
1 teaspoon vanilla extract
1 cup superfine sugar
1 egg
¼ cup brandy
¾ cup roasted blanched almonds, chopped finely
2½ cups all-purpose flour
1½ cups self-raising flour
½ teaspoon ground nutmeg
¼ cup rosewater
½ cup water
3 cups confectioners' sugar

1 Preheat oven to 350°F. Grease oven trays.
2 Beat butter, extract and superfine sugar in small bowl with electric mixer until light and fluffy. Beat in egg and brandy; transfer mixture to large bowl. Stir in nuts and sifted flours and nutmeg, in two batches.
3 Turn dough onto floured surface; knead lightly until smooth. Shape tablespoons of dough into crescent shapes; place about 1 inch apart on trays.
4 Bake about 15 minutes or until browned lightly. Lift hot crescents onto wire racks; brush with combined rosewater and the water. Coat thickly with sifted icing sugar; cool.

prep + cook time 50 minutes
makes 50

chocolate chip cookies

Dark chocolate can be replaced with milk or white chocolate. For choc-nut cookies, replace a third of the chocolate with roasted chopped nuts such as hazelnuts, walnuts, pecans or macadamias. Cookies will keep in an airtight container for up to a week.

8 ounces butter, softened
1 teaspoon vanilla extract
¾ cup superfine sugar
¾ cup firmly packed light brown sugar
1 egg
2¼ cups all-purpose flour
1 teaspoon baking soda
12 ounces dark chocolate melts, chopped coarsely

1 Preheat oven to 350°F. Grease oven trays.
2 Beat butter, extract, sugars and egg in small bowl with electric mixer until light and fluffy. Transfer mixture to large bowl; stir in sifted flour and baking soda, in two batches. Stir in chocolate.
3 Roll tablespoons of mixture into balls; place about 2 inches apart on trays.
4 Bake cookies about 15 minutes; cool on trays.

prep + cook time 30 minutes
makes 36

chocolate chunk and raspberry cookies

Mix and match different colored chocolates with different berries if you like. Store cookies in an airtight container in the fridge for up to a week.

- 4 ounces butter, softened
- ¾ cup firmly packed light brown sugar
- 1 egg
- 1 teaspoon vanilla extract
- 1 cup all-purpose flour
- ¼ cup self-raising flour
- ⅓ cup cocoa powder
- ½ teaspoon baking soda
- 3 ounces dark semi-sweet chocolate, chopped coarsely
- 4 ounces frozen raspberries

1 Preheat oven to 350°F. Line oven trays with parchment paper.
2 Beat butter, sugar, egg and extract in small bowl with electric mixer until combined. Stir in sifted flours, cocoa and baking soda, in two batches, then stir in chocolate and raspberries.
3 Drop tablespoons of mixture about 2 inches apart onto trays; flatten slightly.
4 Bake cookies about 12 minutes. Stand cookies on trays 5 minutes before transferring to a wire rack to cool.

prep + cook time 35 minutes
makes 24

jam drops

Jam drops will keep in an airtight container for up to two days.

4 ounces butter, softened
½ teaspoon vanilla extract
½ cup superfine sugar
1 cup ground almonds
1 egg
1 cup all-purpose flour
1 teaspoon finely grated
  lemon rind
⅓ cup raspberry jam
2 tablespoons apricot jam

1 Preheat oven to 350°F. Line oven trays with parchment paper.
2 Beat butter, extract, sugar and ground almonds in small bowl with electric mixer until light and fluffy. Beat in egg; stir in sifted flour.
3 Divide rind between both jams; mix well.
4 Roll tablespoons of mixture into balls; place about 2 inches apart on trays, flatten slightly. Using end of a wooden spoon, press a flower shape, about ½ inch deep, into dough; fill each hole with a little jam, using raspberry jam for petals of flowers and apricot jam for centers.
5 Bake drops about 15 minutes. Cool on trays.

prep + cook time 40 minutes
makes 24

mocha vanilla twists

Store twists in an airtight container for up to a week.

- 4 ounces butter, softened
- ½ cup superfine sugar
- 1 egg
- 1 teaspoon vanilla extract
- 1⅔ cups all-purpose flour
- 2 teaspoons instant coffee granules
- 2 teaspoons boiling water
- 2 tablespoons cocoa powder

1 Preheat oven to 350°F. Line oven trays with baking paper.
2 Beat butter, sugar, egg and extract in small bowl with electric mixer until combined; stir in sifted flour, in two batches.
3 Divide dough in half. Stir combined coffee and the water and sifted cocoa into one portion to make mocha dough.
4 Divide both dough halves into four equal portions. Roll each portion into a 16-inch sausage. Twist one plain sausage and one mocha sausage together; cut into seven 2-inch lengths. Repeat with remaining plain and mocha dough sausages.
5 Place twists about 1 inch apart on trays.
6 Bake twists about 15 minutes. Cool on trays.

prep + cook time 45 minutes
makes 28

refrigerator slice-and-bake cookies

These basic cookies can be topped with nuts before baking or, once cooked, iced then dipped into various sprinkles, or simply dusted lightly with sifted icing sugar. If you want to flavor the dough, beat any essence or extract of your choice with the butter and sugar mixture, or beat in a teaspoon or two of finely grated citrus rind. The cookies will keep in an airtight container for at least a week.

8 ounces butter, softened
1 cup confectioners' sugar
2½ cups all-purpose flour

1 Beat butter and sifted confectioners' sugar in small bowl with electric mixer until light and fluffy. Transfer to large bowl; stir in sifted flour, in two batches.
2 Knead dough lightly on floured surface until smooth. Divide dough in half; roll each half into a 10-inch log. Wrap logs in plastic; refrigerate about 1 hour or until firm.
3 Preheat oven to 350°F. Grease oven trays.
4 Cut logs into ½-inch slices; place 1 inch apart on trays.
5 Bake cookies about 10 minutes. Cool on trays.

prep + cook time
30 minutes (+ refrigeration)
makes 50

amaretti

These cookies are best if the mixture stands overnight: they will work if they're baked straight away, but they're just not quite as good. Amaretti will keep in an airtight container for at least a week.

2 egg whites
1 cup ground almonds
1 cup superfine sugar
¼ teaspoon almond extract
20 blanched almonds

1 Grease oven trays.
2 Beat egg whites, ground almonds, sugar and extract in small bowl with electric mixer for 3 minutes; stand 5 minutes.
3 Spoon mixture into piping bag fitted with ½ inch plain tube. Pipe mixture onto trays in circular motion, from center out, until about 1½ inches in diameter. Top each amaretti with a nut, cover unbaked amaretti loosely with foil; stand at room temperature overnight (see note).
4 Preheat oven to 350°F.
5 Bake amaretti about 12 minutes. Stand on trays 5 minutes before transferring to a wire rack to cool.

prep + cook time
30 minutes (+ standing)
makes 20

malted milk flowers

Store biscuits in an airtight container for up to a week.

4 ounces butter, softened
½ cup superfine sugar
1 egg
2 tablespoons golden syrup or treacle
⅓ cup malted milk powder
2½ cups all-purpose flour
½ teaspoon baking soda
1½ teaspoons cream of tartar
18 chocolate nonpareils
18 dark chocolate melts

malt icing
1½ cups confectioners' sugar
2 tablespoons malted milk powder
2 tablespoons milk, approximately

1 Beat butter, sugar and egg in small bowl with electric mixer until combined. Transfer mixture to large bowl; stir in golden syrup and sifted dry ingredients, in two batches.
2 Knead dough lightly on floured surface until smooth. Cover; refrigerate 30 minutes.
3 Preheat oven to 300°F. Line oven trays with baking paper.
4 Roll dough between sheets of parchment paper until ¼-inch thick. Cut 3-inch flowers from dough; place flowers about 1 inch apart on trays.
5 Bake cookies about 18 minutes. Cool on trays.
6 Meanwhile, make malt icing.
7 Spread cookies with icing; top half the cookies with nonpareils and remaining cookies with chocolate melts.

malt icing Sift confectioners' sugar and malted milk powder into small heatproof bowl; stir in enough milk to make a thick paste. Stir over small saucepan of simmering water until icing is spreadable.

prep + cook time
50 minutes (+ refrigeration)
makes 36

chocolate wheaties

If the weather is cool, store cookies in an airtight container at room temperature – refrigerate them if the weather is hot.

   3 ounces butter, softened
   ½ cup firmly packed light brown sugar
   1 egg
   ¼ cup desiccated coconut
   ⅓ cup wheat germ
   ⅔ cup wholemeal all-purpose flour
   ⅓ cup white self-raising flour
   6 ounces dark semi-sweet chocolate, melted

1 Beat butter and sugar in small bowl with electric mixer until smooth. Beat in egg until combined. Stir in coconut, wheat germ and sifted flours.
2 Roll dough between sheets of parchment paper until ¼-inch thick. Place on tray; refrigerate 30 minutes.
3 Preheat oven to 350°F. Line oven trays with parchment paper.
4 Cut 3-inch rounds from dough; place rounds about 1 inch apart on trays.
5 Bake wheaties about 20 minutes. Cool on trays.
6 Spread bases of wheaties with chocolate; mark with a fork. Stand at room temperature until set.

prep + cook time 50 minutes (+ refrigeration & standing) makes 18

traditional shortbread

Ground white rice can be used instead of rice flour, although it is slightly coarser in texture. Store shortbread in an airtight container for up to a week.

- 8 ounces butter, softened
- ⅓ cup superfine sugar
- 1 tablespoon water
- 2 cups all-purpose flour
- ½ cup rice flour
- 2 tablespoons granulated sugar

1 Preheat oven to 325°F. Grease oven trays.
2 Beat butter and superfine sugar in medium bowl with electric mixer until light and fluffy; stir in the water and sifted flours, in two batches. Knead mixture on floured surface until smooth.
3 Divide mixture in half; shape each half on separate trays into 8-inch rounds. Mark each round into 12 wedges; prick with fork. Pinch edges of rounds with fingers; sprinkle shortbread with granulated sugar.
4 Bake shortbread about 40 minutes. Stand on trays 5 minutes. Using sharp knife, cut into wedges along marked lines. Cool on trays.

prep + cook time 1 hour
makes 24

melting moments

Unfilled cookies will keep in an airtight container for up to a week. Filled cookies will keep for a few days in an airtight container in the fridge.

8 ounces butter, softened
1 teaspoon vanilla extract
½ cup confectioners' sugar
1½ cups all-purpose flour
½ cup cornstarch

butter cream
3 ounces butter
¾ cup confectioners' sugar
1 teaspoon finely grated lemon rind
1 teaspoon lemon juice

1 Preheat oven to 325°F. Line oven trays with parchment paper.
2 Beat butter, extract and sifted confectioners' sugar in small bowl with electric mixer until light and fluffy. Transfer mixture to large bowl; stir in sifted flours, in two batches.
3 With floured hands, roll rounded teaspoons of mixture into balls; place about 1 inch apart on trays. Flatten slightly with a floured fork.
4 Bake cookies about 15 minutes. Stand on trays 5 minutes before transferring to a wire rack to cool.
5 Make butter cream.
6 Sandwich cookies with butter cream. Dust with extra sifted icing sugar before serving, if you like.

butter cream Beat butter, sifted icing sugar and rind in small bowl with electric mixer until pale and fluffy; beat in juice.

prep + cook time 40 minutes
makes 25

baklava twists

8 ounces butter, softened
¼ cup superfine sugar
1 vanilla extract
1½ cups all-purpose flour
2 teaspoons rosewater

nut topping
⅔ cup roasted unsalted shelled
   pistachios, chopped finely
2 tablespoons honey
3 teaspoons rosewater

1 Make nut topping.
2 Preheat oven to 350°F. Line oven trays with parchment paper.
3 Beat butter, sugar and extract in small bowl with electric mixer until smooth. Transfer mixture to large bowl; stir in sifted flour, in two batches. Stir in rosewater.
4 Roll rounded teaspoons of mixture into balls; roll each ball into 4½-inch log. Twist each log into a loop, overlapping one end over the other. Place twists about 1 inch apart on trays. Top each twist with about ½ teaspoon nut topping.
5 Bake twists about 10 minutes. Cool on trays.

nut topping Combine ingredients in small bowl.

prep + cook time 45 minutes
makes 42

chocolate caramel shortbread cookies

You will need three 4-ounce packets of round shortbread cookies for this recipe. The cookies should be 2¼ inches in diameter. Store filled and chocolate-dipped cookies in an airtight container in the fridge for up to a week.

18 round shortbread cookies
6 ounces dark semi-sweet chocolate, chopped coarsely
2 teaspoons vegetable oil

caramel filling
½ cup firmly packed light brown sugar
2 ounces butter, chopped
2 teaspoons water
1½ tablespoons cornstarch
½ cup milk
1 egg yolk
1 teaspoon vanilla extract

1 Make caramel filling.
2 Spread caramel filling over half the shortbread cookies; top with remaining cookies. Cover; refrigerate 1 hour.
3 Melt chocolate in small heatproof bowl over saucepan of simmering water (do not allow water to touch base of bowl). Remove from heat; stir in oil.
4 Dip one side of cookies in melted chocolate. Stand at room temperature until set.

caramel filling Stir sugar, butter and the water in small saucepan over heat until sugar is dissolved. Stir in blended cornstarch and milk; stir over heat until mixture boils and thickens. Remove from heat; whisk in egg yolk and extract. Cover surface of caramel with plastic wrap; refrigerate 3 hours or overnight.

prep + cook time
25 minutes (+ refrigeration)
makes 9

brandy snaps

Bake the first tray of snaps and while they are cooking prepare the next tray of snaps; put them into the oven as you're getting the first batch out. If you handle four snaps at a time, the process will be easy. Snaps are best made on the day of serving. It is fine to use just one 10 oz. carton of cream for this recipe.

  3 ounces butter
½ cup firmly packed dark brown sugar
⅓ cup golden syrup or treacle
  1 teaspoon ground ginger
⅔ cup all-purpose flour
  1 teaspoon lemon juice
1¼ cups heavy cream, whipped

1 Preheat oven to 350°F. Grease oven trays.
2 Stir butter, sugar, syrup and ginger in medium saucepan, over low heat, until smooth. Remove from heat; stir in sifted flour and juice.
3 Drop rounded teaspoons of mixture about 2 inches apart onto trays. Using a wet, thin metal spatula, spread mixture into 3¼-inch rounds.
4 Bake snaps about 8 minutes or until bubbling and golden brown. Working quickly, slide a thin metal spatula under each snap; shape each one into a cone. Place on wire rack to cool. Fill with whipped cream just before serving.

prep + cook time 40 minutes
makes 32

spicy fruit mince pillows

Pillows will keep in an airtight container at room temperature for up to a week.

 3 ounces butter, softened
 ⅓ cup confectioners' sugar
 1 egg
 1¼ cups all-purpose flour
 ¼ cup self-raising flour
 2 tablespoons milk
 2 teaspoons superfine sugar

spicy fruit filling
 2⅔ cups seeded dried dates, chopped coarsely
 ¾ cup water
 2 teaspoons ground allspice
 ¼ teaspoon ground cloves
pinch baking soda

1 Beat butter and sifted icing sugar in small bowl with electric mixer until smooth. Beat in egg until combined. Stir in sifted flours, in two batches. Cover dough; refrigerate 30 minutes.
2 Meanwhile, make spicy fruit filling.
3 Preheat oven to 350°F. Line oven trays with parchment paper.
4 Roll dough between sheets of parchment paper to 12-inch x 16-inch rectangle; cut into four 3-inch x 16-inch strips.
5 Spoon filling into piping bag fitted with large ¾-inch plain tube; pipe filling down center of each strip. Fold edges in until they meet to enclose filling; turn seam-side down onto board. Cut each roll into 10 pillow shapes; place pillows, seam-side down, on trays; brush with milk, sprinkle with superfine sugar.
6 Bake pillows about 20 minutes. Cool on trays.

spicy fruit filling Place dates and the water in medium saucepan; cook, stirring, about 10 minutes or until thick and smooth. Stir in spices and baking soda. Cool.

prep + cook time
50 minutes (+ refrigeration)
makes 40

lime and ginger kisses

Unfilled cookies will keep in an airtight container for up to a week. Filled cookies will keep for a few days in an airtight container in the fridge.

- 4 ounces butter, softened
- ½ cup firmly packed light brown sugar
- 1 egg
- ¼ cup all-purpose flour
- ¼ cup self-raising flour
- ¾ cup cornstarch
- 2 teaspoons ground ginger
- ½ teaspoon ground cinnamon
- ¼ teaspoon ground cloves

lime butter cream
- 2 ounces butter, softened
- 2 teaspoons finely grated lime rind
- ¾ cup confectioners' sugar
- 2 teaspoons milk

1 Preheat oven to 350°F. Line oven trays with parchment paper.
2 Beat butter, sugar and egg in small bowl with electric mixer until smooth. Stir in sifted dry ingredients.
3 Roll heaped teaspoons of mixture into balls; place balls about 2 inches apart on trays.
4 Bake cookies about 10 minutes. Loosen cookies; cool on trays.
5 Meanwhile, make lime butter cream.
6 Sandwich cookies with butter cream.

lime butter cream Beat butter and rind in small bowl with electric mixer until as white as possible. Beat in sifted icing sugar and milk, in two batches.

prep + cook time
35 minutes (+ cooling)
makes 18

hazelnut moments
with choc berry filling

Unfilled cookies will keep in an airtight container for up to a week. Filled cookies will keep for a few days in an airtight container in the fridge.

  3 ounces butter, softened
 ½ teaspoon vanilla extract
 ¼ cup superfine sugar
  1 egg
 ½ cup ground hazelnuts
 ¾ cup all-purpose flour
 ¼ cup cocoa powder

choc berry filling
  3 ounces dark semi-sweet
    chocolate, melted
  2 ounces butter, softened
 ⅓ cup chocolate hazelnut
    spread
 ¼ cup fresh raspberries,
    chopped coarsely

1 Beat butter, extract, sugar and egg in small bowl with electric mixer until combined. Stir in ground hazelnuts, then sifted flour and cocoa.
2 Divide dough in half; roll each half between sheets of parchment paper until ⅛-inch thick. Refrigerate 30 minutes.
3 Preheat oven to 350°F. Line oven trays with parchment paper.
4 Cut dough into 1½-inch fluted rounds; place on trays 1 inch apart.
5 Bake cookies about 8 minutes. Cool on trays.
6 Make choc berry filling.
7 Spoon choc berry filling into piping bag fitted with ¾-inch fluted tube. Pipe filling onto flat side of half the cookies; top with remaining cookies.

choc berry filling Beat cooled chocolate, butter and spread in small bowl with electric mixer until thick and glossy. Fold in raspberries.

prep + cook time 30 minutes (+ refrigeration & cooling)
makes 24

coconut chocolate crunchies

Unfilled cookies will keep in an airtight container for up to a week. Filled cookies will keep for a few days in an airtight container in the fridge.

4 ounces butter, softened
¾ cup firmly packed light brown sugar
1 tablespoon golden syrup or treacle
2 eggs
2 cups self-raising flour
1 cup desiccated coconut
½ cup quick-cooking oats

milk chocolate ganache
6 ounces milk chocolate, chopped coarsely
1 ounce butter

1 Preheat oven to 350°F. Line oven trays with parchment paper.
2 Beat butter, sugar and syrup in small bowl with electric mixer until smooth. Beat in eggs, one at a time. Stir in sifted flour, coconut and oats.
3 Roll rounded teaspoons of mixture into balls; place about 2 inches apart on trays. Flatten with fork.
4 Bake cookies about 12 minutes. Cool on trays.
5 Meanwhile, make milk chocolate ganache.
6 Sandwich cookies with ganache; refrigerate until firm.

milk chocolate ganache Stir chocolate and butter in small heatproof bowl over small saucepan of simmering water until smooth; cool.

prep + cook time 40 minutes (+ refrigeration & cooling) makes 40

wagonettes

You need two 6½-ounce packets of milk chocolate wheaten cookies for this recipe. If the marshmallow sets too quickly, return it to the mixer bowl with about 1 tablespoon boiling water and beat it for about a minute. Unfilled cookies will keep in an airtight container for up to a week. Filled cookies will keep for a few days in an airtight container in the fridge.

⅓ cup superfine sugar
⅓ cup water
 2 teaspoons gelatin
⅓ cup strawberry jam,
    warmed, strained
32 milk chocolate wheaten
    cookies
½ teaspoon vanilla extract
pink food coloring

1 Stir sugar and half the water in small saucepan over low heat until sugar dissolves.
2 Combine gelatin and the remaining water in small jug. Pour gelatin mixture into hot sugar syrup; stir over medium heat about 3 minutes or until gelatine dissolves. Pour mixture into small heatproof bowl; cool.
3 Spread jam onto the plain side of half the cookies.
4 To make marshmallow, beat gelatin mixture in small bowl with electric mixer on high speed about 8 minutes or until very thick. Beat in extract and a few drops of food coloring.
5 Spoon marshmallow into piping bag fitted with ¾-inch plain tube. Pipe marshmallow over jam; top with remaining cookies.

prep + cook time
30 minutes (+ cooling)
makes 16

passionfruit meringue kisses

2 egg whites
½ cup superfine sugar
yellow food coloring
1 teaspoon strained
   passionfruit juice
1 teaspoon cornstarch

passionfruit butter
2 ounces unsalted butter,
   softened
¾ cup confectioners' sugar
1 tablespoon passionfruit pulp

1 Preheat oven to 250°F.
Grease oven trays; line with
parchment paper.
2 Beat egg whites, sugar and
a few drops of food coloring in
small bowl with electric mixer
about 15 minutes or until sugar
dissolves. Fold in juice and
cornstarch.
3 Spoon meringue mixture into
piping bag fitted with ¾-inch
fluted tube; pipe 1½-inch stars
onto trays ¾ inch apart.
4 Bake meringues about 1 hour.
Cool on trays.
5 Meanwhile, make passionfruit
butter.
6 Sandwich meringues with
passionfruit butter.

passionfruit butter Beat butter
and sifted confectioners' sugar
in small bowl with electric mixer
until light and fluffy. Stir in pulp.

prep + cook time
1 hour 25 minutes (+ cooling)
makes 24

pistachio, white chocolate and honey french macaroons

⅓ cup roasted unsalted shelled pistachios
3 egg whites
¼ cup superfine sugar
green food coloring
1¼ cups confectioners' sugar
¾ cup ground almonds

honeyed white chocolate ganache
¼ cup pouring cream
5 ounces white chocolate, chopped coarsely
2 teaspoons honey

1 Preheat oven to 300°F. Grease oven trays; line with parchment paper.
2 Process nuts until finely ground.
3 Beat egg whites in small bowl with electric mixer until soft peaks form. Add superfine sugar and few drops food coloring, beat until sugar dissolves. Transfer mixture to large bowl; fold in ¼ cup of the ground pistachios, sifted icing sugar and ground almonds, in two batches.
4 Spoon mixture into piping bag fitted with ½-inch plain tube. Pipe 1½-inch rounds about 1 inch apart onto trays. Tap trays on bench so macaroons spread slightly. Sprinkle macaroons with remaining ground pistachios; stand 30 minutes.

5 Bake macaroons about 20 minutes. Cool on trays.
6 Meanwhile, make honeyed white chocolate ganache.
7 Sandwich macaroons with ganache.

honeyed white chocolate ganache Bring cream to the boil in small saucepan. Remove from heat; pour over chocolate and honey in small bowl, stir until smooth. Stand at room temperature until spreadable.

prep + cook time
45 minutes (+ standing)
makes 16

chocolate french macaroons

Buttered brazil nuts are toffee-coated nuts; they're available from nut shops and gourmet food stores.

3 egg whites
¼ cup superfine sugar
1¼ cups confectioners' sugar
¾ cup ground almonds
¼ cup cocoa powder

dark chocolate ganache
¼ cup pouring cream
5 ounces dark semi-sweet chocolate, chopped coarsely
1 tablespoon finely crushed buttered brazil nuts

1 Preheat oven to 300°F. Grease oven trays; line with baking paper.
2 Beat egg whites in small bowl with electric mixer until soft peaks form. Add superfine sugar; beat until sugar dissolves. Transfer mixture to large bowl. Fold in sifted confectioners' sugar, ground almonds and sifted cocoa, in two batches.
3 Spoon mixture into piping bag fitted with ½-inch plain tube. Pipe 1½-inch rounds about 1 inch apart onto trays. Tap trays on bench so macaroons spread slightly. Stand 30 minutes.
4 Bake macaroons about 20 minutes. Cool on trays.

5 Meanwhile, make dark chocolate ganache.
6 Sandwich macaroons with ganache.

dark chocolate ganache
Bring cream to the boil in small saucepan. Remove from heat; pour over chocolate in small bowl, stir until smooth. Stir in nuts. Stand at room temperature until spreadable.

prep + cook time
45 minutes (+ standing)
makes 16

coconut french macaroons

3 egg whites
¼ cup superfine sugar
½ teaspoon coconut essence
1¼ cups confectioners' sugar
¾ cup ground almonds
¼ cup desiccated coconut
1 tablespoon confectioners'
   sugar, extra

white chocolate ganache
¼ cup pouring cream
5 ounces white chocolate,
   chopped coarsely
2 teaspoons coconut-flavored
   liqueur

1 Preheat oven to 300°F. Grease oven trays; line with parchment paper.
2 Beat egg whites in small bowl with electric mixer until soft peaks form. Add superfine sugar and essence, beat until sugar dissolves; transfer mixture to large bowl. Fold in sifted confectioners' sugar, ground almonds and coconut, in two batches.
3 Spoon mixture into piping bag fitted with ½-inch plain tube. Pipe 1½-inch rounds about 1 inch apart onto trays. Tap trays on bench so macaroons spread slightly. Stand 30 minutes.
4 Bake macaroons about 20 minutes. Cool on trays.

5 Meanwhile, make white chocolate ganache.
6 Sandwich macaroons with ganache. Serve dusted with extra sifted confectioners' sugar.

white chocolate ganache
Bring cream to the boil in small saucepan. Remove from heat; pour over chocolate in small bowl, stir until smooth. Stir in liqueur. Stand at room temperature until spreadable.

prep + cook time
45 minutes (+ standing)
makes 16

strawberry french macaroons

3 egg whites
¼ cup superfine sugar
pink food coloring
2 large fresh or frozen
  strawberries
1¼ cups confectioners' sugar
1 cup ground almonds
⅓ cup strawberry jam
1 tablespoon confectioners'
  sugar, extra

1 Preheat oven to 300°F. Grease oven trays; line with baking paper.
2 Beat egg whites in small bowl with electric mixer until soft peaks form. Add superfine sugar and few drops food coloring, beat until sugar dissolves. Transfer mixture to large bowl.
3 Meanwhile, push fresh strawberries (or thawed frozen berries) through a fine sieve; you need 1 tablespoon of strawberry puree.
4 Fold sifted confectioners' sugar, ground almonds and strawberry puree into egg white mixture, in two batches.

5 Spoon mixture into piping bag fitted with ½-inch plain tube. Pipe 1½-inch rounds about 1 inch apart onto trays. Tap trays on bench so macaroons spread slightly. Stand 30 minutes.
6 Bake macaroons about 20 minutes. Cool on trays.
7 Sandwich macaroons with jam. Dust with extra sifted confectioners' sugar.

prep + cook time
40 minutes (+ standing)
makes 16

monte carlos

6 ounces unsalted butter,
    softened
1 teaspoon vanilla extract
½ cup firmly packed light
    brown sugar
1 egg
1¼ cups self-raising flour
¾ cup all-purpose flour
½ cup desiccated coconut
½ cup raspberry jam

cream filling
2 ounces unsalted butter,
    softened
¾ cup confectioners' sugar
½ teaspoon vanilla extract
2 teaspoons milk

1 Preheat oven to 325°F. Grease oven trays.
2 Beat butter, extract and sugar in small bowl with electric mixer until light and fluffy. Add egg, beat until combined. Stir in sifted flours and coconut.
3 Shape level teaspoons of dough into oval shapes; place about 1½ inches apart on trays. Rough surface with fork.
4 Bake cookies about 12 minutes. Cool on trays.
5 Meanwhile, make cream filling.
6 Place ½ teaspoon each of jam and cream filling in center of half the cookies; top with remaining cookies, gently press together.

cream filling Beat butter and sifted confectioners' sugar in small bowl with electric mixer until light and fluffy. Beat in extract and milk.

prep + cook time 50 minutes
makes 50

passionfruit cream biscuits

You need about six passionfruit for this recipe.

- 4 ounces butter, softened
- 2 teaspoons finely grated lemon rind
- ⅓ cup superfine sugar
- 2 tablespoons golden syrup or treacle
- 1 cup self-raising flour
- ⅔ cup all-purpose flour
- ¼ cup passionfruit pulp

passionfruit cream

- 2 tablespoons passionfruit pulp
- 3 ounces butter, softened
- 1 cup confectioners' sugar

1 Beat butter, rind and sugar in small bowl with electric mixer until light and fluffy. Add golden syrup, beat until combined. Stir in sifted flours and pulp.

2 Turn dough onto floured surface, knead gently until smooth. Cut dough in half; roll each portion between sheets of parchment paper to ¼-inch thickness. Refrigerate 30 minutes.

3 Preheat oven to 350°F. Grease oven trays; line with parchment paper.

4 Cut 25 x 1½-inch fluted rounds from each portion of dough; place about 1 inch apart on trays.

5 Bake cookies about 10 minutes. Cool on trays.

6 Meanwhile, make passionfruit cream.

7 Spoon passionfruit cream into piping bag fitted with ¼-inch fluted tube. Pipe cream onto half the cookies; top with remaining biscuits. Serve dusted with a little extra sifted confectioners' sugar, if you like.

passionfruit cream Strain passionfruit pulp through fine sieve into small jug, discard seeds. Beat butter and sugar in small bowl with electric mixer until light and fluffy. Beat in passionfruit juice.

prep + cook time 45 minutes (+ refrigeration & cooling) makes 25

hazelnut pinwheels

Store pinwheels in an airtight container for up to a week.

1¼ cups all-purpose flour
3 ounces cold butter, chopped
½ cup superfine sugar
1 egg yolk
1 tablespoon milk, approximately
⅓ cup chocolate hazelnut spread
2 tablespoons ground hazelnuts

1 Process flour, butter and sugar until crumbly. Add egg yolk; process with enough milk until mixture forms a ball. Knead dough on floured surface until smooth. Wrap in plastic; refrigerate 1 hour.
2 Roll dough between sheets of baking paper into a 8-inch x 12-inch rectangle; remove top sheet of paper. Spread dough evenly with spread; sprinkle with ground hazelnuts. Using bottom sheet of paper as a guide, roll dough tightly from one long side to enclose filling. Wrap roll in plastic; refrigerate 30 minutes.

3 Preheat oven to 350°F. Grease oven trays; line with parchment paper.
4 Remove plastic from dough. Cut roll into ½-inch slices; place on trays ¾ inch apart.
5 Bake pinwheels about 20 minutes. Stand on trays 5 minutes before transferring to a wire rack to cool.

prep + cook time
40 minutes (+ refrigeration)
makes 30

linzer cookies

The 1-inch fluted center rounds can be baked for about 10 minutes; sandwich with extra jam. You can substitute the fig and ginger jam for any jam of your choice. These cookies are best served on the day they are made. Store unfilled cookies in an airtight container for up to a week.

⅔ cup all-purpose flour
⅔ cup superfine sugar
1½ cups finely chopped walnuts
1 hard-boiled egg yolk
3 ounces butter, chopped coarsely
1 egg yolk
⅔ cup fig and ginger jam
1 tablespoon confectioners' sugar

1 Combine sifted flour, superfine sugar, nuts and hard-boiled egg yolk in medium bowl; rub in butter. Stir in egg yolk until ingredients come together.
2 Turn dough onto floured surface, knead gently until smooth. Divide dough in half; roll each portion between sheets of parchment paper to ⅛-inch thickness. Refrigerate 30 minutes.
3 Preheat oven to 325°F. Grease oven trays; line with parchment paper.
4 Cut 24 x 2-inch fluted rounds from each portion of dough; place about 1 inch apart on trays. Cut 1-inch fluted rounds from center of half the rounds.
5 Bake cookies about 15 minutes. Cool on trays.
6 Sandwich cookies with jam. Serve dusted with sifted confectioners' sugar.

prep + cook time 50 minutes
(+ refrigeration & cooling)
makes 24

coffee almond cookies

Store in an airtight container for up to a week.

- 1 tablespoon instant coffee granules
- 3 teaspoons hot water
- 3 cups ground almonds
- 1 cup superfine sugar
- 2 tablespoons coffee-flavored liqueur
- 3 egg whites, beaten lightly
- 24 coffee beans

1 Preheat oven to 350°F. Grease oven trays; line with parchment paper.
2 Dissolve coffee in the hot water in a large bowl. Stir in ground almonds, sugar, liqueur and egg whites until mixture forms a firm paste.
3 Roll level tablespoons of mixture into balls; place on trays 1¼ inches apart; flatten with hand. Press coffee beans into tops of cookies.
4 Bake cookies about 15 minutes. Cool on trays.

prep + cook time 30 minutes
makes 24

vanilla bean thins

1 vanilla bean
1 ounce butter, softened
¼ cup superfine sugar
1 egg white, beaten lightly
¼ cup all-purpose flour

1 Preheat oven to 400°F. Grease oven trays; line with parchment paper.

2 Halve vanilla bean lengthways; scrape seeds into medium bowl, discard pod. Add butter and sugar to bowl; stir until combined. Stir in egg white and sifted flour.

3 Spoon mixture into piping bag fitted with ¼-inch plain tube. Pipe 2¼-inch long strips (making them slightly wider at both ends) about 2 inches apart on trays.

4 Bake cookies about 5 minutes or until edges are browned lightly. Cool on trays.

prep + cook time 25 minutes
makes 24

chocolate lace crisps

3 ounces dark semi-sweet
  chocolate, chopped coarsely
2½ ounces butter, chopped
1 cup superfine sugar
1 egg, beaten lightly
1 cup all-purpose flour
2 tablespoons cocoa powder
¼ teaspoon baking soda
¼ cup confectioners' sugar

1 Melt chocolate and butter in small saucepan over low heat. Transfer to medium bowl.

2 Stir in superfine sugar, egg and sifted flour, cocoa and baking soda. Cover; refrigerate 15 minutes or until mixture is firm enough to handle.

3 Preheat oven to 350°F. Grease oven trays; line with parchment paper.

4 Roll level tablespoons of mixture into balls; roll each ball in icing sugar, place on trays 3¼ inches apart.

5 Bake crisps about 15 minutes. Cool on trays.

prep + cook time
45 minutes (+ refrigeration)
makes 24

Slices

These slices are richer and more luscious than usual. They're special afternoon tea slices, filled with caramel or fruit, spread with tart lemon icing or drizzled with melted chocolate. If you are serving a lot of rich food cut these into smaller slices – just one mouthful will be enough.

chocolate caramel slice

The slice will keep in an airtight container in the refrigerator for up to 4 days.

½ cup self-raising flour
½ cup all-purpose flour
1 cup desiccated coconut
1 cup firmly packed light brown sugar
4 ounces butter, melted
14 ounces canned sweetened condensed milk
1 ounce butter, extra
2 tablespoons golden syrup or treacle
6 ounces dark semi-sweet chocolate, chopped coarsely
2 teaspoons vegetable oil

1 Preheat oven to 350°F. Grease 8-inch x 12-inch rectangular pan; line base and long sides with parchment paper, extending paper 2 inches over sides.
2 Combine sifted flours, coconut, sugar and butter in medium bowl; press mixture evenly over base of pan.
3 Bake about 15 minutes or until browned lightly.
4 Meanwhile, make caramel filling by combining condensed milk, extra butter and syrup in small saucepan. Stir over medium heat about 15 minutes or until caramel mixture is golden brown; pour over base. Bake 10 minutes; cool.

5 Make topping by combining chocolate and oil in small saucepan; stir over low heat until smooth. Pour warm topping over cold caramel. Refrigerate 3 hours or overnight.

prep + cook time 45 minutes (+ cooling & refrigeration)
makes 24

rich hazelnut slice

Slice will keep in an airtight container in the refrigerator for up to a week.

8 ounces plain chocolate cookies
¾ cup roasted hazelnuts, chopped coarsely
5 ounces unsalted butter, melted
14 ounces canned sweetened condensed milk
12 ounces milk chocolate, chopped coarsely
10 ounces dark semi-sweet chocolate, chopped coarsely
½ ounce unsalted butter, extra
1 ounce white chocolate, melted

1 Grease 8-inch x 12-inch rectangular pan; line base and long sides with parchment paper, extending paper 2 inches over sides.
2 Process cookies and ¼ cup of the nuts until fine; add butter, process until combined. Press mixture over base of pan. Refrigerate about 20 minutes or until firm.
3 Stir condensed milk and 11 ounces of the milk chocolate in small saucepan over low heat until smooth. Stir in remaining nuts. Working quickly, spread chocolate mixture over base.
4 Stir dark chocolate and extra butter in small saucepan over low heat until smooth. Spread over milk chocolate layer.
5 Melt remaining milk chocolate; drizzle milk and white chocolate over slice. Refrigerate 20 minutes or until firm.

prep + cook time
30 minutes (+ refrigeration)
makes 32

fruity choc chip slice

Slice can be stored in an airtight container for up to a week.

- ⅓ cup firmly packed light brown sugar
- 3 ounces butter, chopped coarsely
- 1¼ cups all-purpose flour
- 1 egg yolk

fruity choc chip topping

- 2 eggs
- 1 cup firmly packed light brown sugar
- ⅓ cup self-raising flour
- 1 cup milk choc bits
- 1 cup rolled oats
- ½ cup shredded coconut
- ⅓ cup coarsely chopped, roasted unsalted shelled pistachios
- ½ cup finely chopped dried mixed berries
- ½ cup finely chopped dried apple

1 Preheat oven to 350°F. Grease 8-inch x 12-inch rectangular pan; line base and long sides with parchment paper, extending paper 2 inches over sides.
2 Stir sugar and butter in medium saucepan over low heat until smooth. Remove from heat; stir in sifted flour then egg yolk. Press mixture firmly over base of pan.
3 Bake about 10 minutes or until browned lightly. Cool.
4 Meanwhile, make fruity choc chip topping.
5 Spread topping over base; bake about 25 minutes or until browned lightly. Cool in pan.

fruity choc chip topping Beat eggs and sugar in small bowl with electric mixer until thick and pale, transfer to large bowl; fold in sifted flour then remaining ingredients.

prep + cook time 1 hour
makes 24

choc nut and cornflake slice

4 ounces butter,
chopped coarsely
½ cup superfine sugar
⅓ cup light corn syrup
⅓ cup crunchy peanut butter
4 cups cornflakes
11 ounces milk chocolate,
melted

1 Grease 8-inch x 12-inch rectangular pan; line base and long sides with parchment paper, extending paper 2 inches over sides.

2 Stir butter, sugar, corn syrup and peanut butter in large saucepan over low heat until sugar dissolves. Bring to the boil. Reduce heat; simmer, uncovered, without stirring, 5 minutes. Gently stir in cornflakes. Spread mixture into pan; press firmly. Refrigerate about 30 minutes or until set.

3 Spread chocolate over slice; stand at room temperature until set.

prep + cook time
30 minutes (+ refrigeration)
makes 24

raspberry coconut slice

Slice can be stored in an airtight container for up to a week.

- 3 ounces butter, softened
- ½ cup superfine sugar
- 1 egg
- ¼ cup self-raising flour
- ⅔ cup all-purpose flour
- 1 tablespoon custard powder
- ⅔ cup raspberry jam

coconut topping
- 2 cups desiccated coconut
- ¼ cup superfine sugar
- 2 eggs, beaten lightly

1 Preheat oven to 350°F. Grease 8-inch x 12-inch rectangular pan; line base and long sides with parchment paper, extending paper 2 inches over sides.
2 Beat butter, sugar and egg in small bowl with electric mixer until light and fluffy. Transfer to medium bowl; stir in sifted flours and custard powder. Spread dough into pan; spread with jam.
3 Make coconut topping; sprinkle over jam.
4 Bake slice about 40 minutes; cool in pan.

coconut topping Combine ingredients in medium bowl.

prep + cook time 1 hour
makes 16

lattice slice with passionfruit icing

You need to buy two packets of lattice cookies for this recipe. The slice will keep in an airtight container in the refrigerator for up to 4 days.

- 2 teaspoons gelatin
- 2 tablespoons water
- 8 ounces cream cheese, softened
- 8 ounces unsalted butter, softened
- ½ cup superfine sugar
- 1 teaspoon vanilla extract
- 2 tablespoons lemon juice
- 35 square lattice cookies

passionfruit icing
- 2 cups confectioners' sugar
- 2 teaspoons unsalted butter
- 2 tablespoons passionfruit pulp
- 2 teaspoons hot water, approximately

1 Grease 8-inch x 12-inch rectangular pan; line base and long sides with parchment paper, extending paper 2 inches over sides.
2 Sprinkle gelatin over the water in small heatproof jug; stand jug in small saucepan of simmering water, stir until gelatin dissolves.
3 Beat cream cheese, butter, sugar and extract in small bowl with electric mixer until smooth. Stir in juice and gelatin mixture.
4 Line base of pan with half the biscuits; trim cookies to fit, if necessary. Spread cream cheese filling evenly over cookie base; top with remaining cookies.
5 Make passionfruit icing.
6 Spread icing over cookies. Refrigerate 3 hours or overnight.

passionfruit icing Sift confectioners' sugar into small heatproof bowl; stir in butter, passionfruit and enough of the water to make a thick paste. Place bowl over small saucepan of simmering water; stir until icing is spreadable.

prep + cook time
30 minutes (+ refrigeration)
makes 12

chocolate peanut slice

When beating sugar into the egg white, beat only until combined; the sugar will not dissolve at this stage. Slice can be stored in an airtight container in the refrigerator for a week.

1½ sheets shortcrust pastry
⅔ cup raspberry jam
3 egg whites
1½ cups superfine sugar
1 cup plain cake crumbs
⅓ cup cocoa powder
1 teaspoon vanilla extract
1¾ cups roasted unsalted peanuts
2 teaspoons confectioners' sugar

1 Preheat oven to 400°F.
2 Place pastry sheets on flat oven tray, prick all over with a fork; bake about 10 minutes or until pastry is browned lightly and almost cooked through. Place hot pastry pieces, side-by-side, on flat surface; using base of a 8-inch x 12-inch rectangular pan as a guide, cut pastry to fit pan. Grease and line base and sides of pan; place trimmed pastry into base of pan. Spread pastry evenly with jam.
3 Reduce oven to 350°F.
4 Beat egg whites in small bowl with electric mixer until firm peaks form. Beat in sugar in three batches. Stir in cake crumbs, sifted cocoa, extract then nuts. Spread nut mixture evenly over jam.
5 Bake slice about 40 minutes. Cool in pan before cutting. Dust with sifted confectioners' sugar before serving.

prep + cook time
1 hour (+ cooling)
makes 30

apple streusel slice

Slice will keep in an airtight container in the refrigerator for up to 3 days.

  7 ounces unsalted butter, softened
  1 cup superfine sugar
  2 egg yolks
1⅓ cups all-purpose flour
  ½ cup self-raising flour
  2 tablespoons custard powder
  4 large apples, sliced thinly
  1 tablespoon honey
  1 teaspoon finely grated lemon rind

streusel topping
  ½ cup all-purpose flour
  ¼ cup self-raising flour
  ⅓ cup firmly packed light brown sugar
  ½ teaspoon ground cinnamon
  3 ounces unsalted butter, chopped coarsely

1 Make streusel topping.
2 Preheat oven to 350°F. Grease 8-inch x 12-inch rectangular pan; line base and long sides with parchment paper, extending paper 2 inches over sides.
3 Beat butter, sugar and egg yolks in small bowl with electric mixer until light and fluffy, transfer to large bowl; stir in sifted flours and custard powder. Press mixture into pan.
4 Bake 25 minutes. Cool in pan 15 minutes.
5 Meanwhile, cook apple, honey and rind, covered, in medium saucepan, stirring occasionally, about 5 minutes or until apples are tender. Remove from heat; drain, cool 15 minutes.
6 Spread apple mixture over base; coarsely grate streusel topping over apple.
7 Bake slice about 20 minutes. Cool slice in pan.

streusel topping Process ingredients until combined. Wrap in plastic; freeze 1 hour or until firm.

prep + cook time
1 hour (+ freezing & cooling)
makes 12

chocolate brownie slice

4 ounces butter, chopped coarsely
6 ounces dark semi-sweet chocolate, chopped coarsely
½ cup superfine sugar
2 eggs
1¼ cups all-purpose flour
5 ounces white chocolate, chopped coarsely
3 ounces milk chocolate, chopped coarsely

1 Preheat oven to 350°F. Grease deep 8-inch square cake pan; line base with parchment paper, extending paper 2 inches over sides.

2 Stir butter and dark chocolate in medium saucepan over low heat until smooth. Remove from heat; cool 10 minutes.

3 Stir in sugar and eggs, then sifted flour, white chocolate and milk chocolate. Spread mixture into pan.

4 Bake slice about 35 minutes. Cool in pan.

prep + cook time 1 hour
makes 25

fruit mince slice

Use granulated sugar instead of the demerara, if you like. Slice can be stored in an airtight container for up to a week.

1½ cups all-purpose flour
1¼ cups self-raising flour
5 ounces cold butter, chopped
1 tablespoon golden syrup or treacle
1 egg
⅓ cup milk, approximately
2 teaspoons milk, extra
1 tablespoon demerara sugar

fruit mince
1 pound mixed dried fruit, chopped coarsely
½ cup water
½ cup firmly packed dark brown sugar
1 tablespoon orange marmalade
2 teaspoons finely grated orange rind
2 tablespoons orange juice

1 Make fruit mince.
2 Grease 8-inch x 12-inch rectangular pan; line base and long sides with parchment paper, extending paper 2 inches) over sides.
3 Sift flours into large bowl; rub in butter until mixture is crumbly. Stir in combined syrup and egg with enough milk to make a firm dough. Knead dough gently on floured surface until smooth. Refrigerate 30 minutes.
4 Preheat oven to 400°F.
5 Divide dough in half. Roll one half between sheets of parchment paper until large enough to cover base of pan; press into pan. Spread fruit mince over dough.
6 Roll remaining dough between sheets of parchment paper until large enough to cover fruit mince; place on top of fruit mince, trim to fit. Brush with extra milk; sprinkle with sugar.
7 Bake slice about 20 minutes. Cool in pan before cutting.

fruit mince Cook ingredients in medium saucepan, stirring, over medium heat, about 10 minutes or until thick. Cool.

prep + cook time 50 minutes (+ refrigeration & cooling)
makes 24

white chocolate and berry cheesecake slice

It is fine to use just one 10 oz. carton of cream for this recipe.

8 ounces butternut snap cookies
2 teaspoons gelatin
¼ cup boiling water
12 ounces softened cream cheese
⅓ cup superfine sugar
1¼ cups pouring cream
6 ounces white chocolate, melted
4 ounces frozen mixed berries
3 ounces frozen mixed berries, extra

1 Grease deep 8-inch square loose-based cake pan.
2 Place cookies in base of pan.
3 Sprinkle gelatin over water in small heatproof jug; stand jug in small saucepan of simmering water, stir until gelatin dissolves. Cool 5 minutes.
4 Meanwhile, beat cream cheese and sugar in small bowl with electric mixer until smooth; beat in cream. Stir in gelatin mixture, chocolate and berries. Pour filling into pan; sprinkle with extra berries.
5 Refrigerate slice 3 hours or overnight.

prep + cook time
30 minutes (+ refrigeration)
makes 20

lime and coconut slice

7½ ounces plain sweet cookies
½ cup sweetened condensed
  milk
3 ounces unsalted butter,
  chopped
1 teaspoon finely grated
  lime rind
1 tablespoon lime juice
½ cup shredded coconut

lime icing
2 cups confectioners' sugar
½ ounce unsalted butter,
  melted
2 tablespoons lime juice

1 Grease 8-inch x 12-inch
rectangular pan; line base
and long sides with parchment
paper, extending paper 2 inches
over sides.
2 Process 6 ounces of the
cookies until fine; chop
remaining cookies coarsely.
3 Stir condensed milk and
butter in small saucepan over
medium heat until smooth.
4 Combine processed and
chopped cookies, rind, juice
and coconut in medium bowl.
Add condensed milk mixture;
stir to combine.
5 Press mixture firmly into pan.
Refrigerate 30 minutes or
until firm.
6 Meanwhile, make lime icing.
7 Spread icing over slice.
Refrigerate 30 minutes or
until firm.

lime icing Sift confectioners'
sugar into small heatproof bowl;
stir in butter, juice and enough
water to make a thick paste.
Place bowl over small saucepan
of simmering water, stir until
icing is spreadable.

prep + cook time
25 minutes (+ refrigeration)
makes 24

bakewell slice

Slice can be stored in an airtight container for up to a week.

5 ounces unsalted butter, softened
¼ cup superfine sugar
2 egg yolks
1½ cups all-purpose flour
¾ cup ground almonds
¾ cup strawberry jam

almond filling

6 ounces unsalted butter, softened
1 teaspoon finely grated lemon rind
¾ cup superfine sugar
3 eggs
1¼ cups ground almonds
¼ cup all-purpose flour

lemon icing

2 cups confectioners' sugar
¼ cup lemon juice, approximately

1 Beat butter, sugar and egg yolks in small bowl with electric mixer until combined. Stir in sifted flour and ground almonds, in two batches. Knead pastry gently on floured surface until smooth. Wrap in plastic; refrigerate 30 minutes.
2 Make almond filling.
3 Meanwhile, preheat oven to 400°F.
4 Grease 8-inch x 12-inch rectangular pan; line base and long sides with parchment paper, extending paper 2 inches over sides. Roll out pastry between sheets of parchment paper until large enough to line pan; press into base and sides, trim edge. Spread jam then almond filling evenly over base.
5 Bake about 30 minutes. Cool in pan.
6 Make lemon icing.
7 Spread lemon icing over slice; stand at room temperature until icing is set.

almond filling Beat butter, rind and sugar in small bowl with electric mixer until light and fluffy. Beat in eggs, one at a time. Stir in ground almonds and sifted flour.

lemon icing Sift confectioners sugar into small bowl; stir in enough of the juice until icing is spreadable.

prep + cook time
1 hour 10 minutes
(+ refrigeration & standing)
makes 32

hedgehog slice

We used plain sweet shortbread biscuits.

14 ounces canned sweetened condensed milk
3 ounces unsalted butter, chopped coarsely
6 ounces dark semi-sweet chocolate, chopped coarsely
8 ounces plain sweet cookies
⅔ cup roasted hazelnuts
⅔ cup sultanas

1 Grease 8-inch x 12-inch rectangular pan; line base and long sides with parchment paper, extending paper 2 inches over sides.
2 Stir condensed milk and butter in medium saucepan over medium heat until smooth. Remove from heat; add chocolate, stir until smooth.
3 Break cookies into small pieces; place in large bowl with nuts and sultanas. Stir in chocolate mixture.
4 Press mixture firmly into pan. Refrigerate 2 hours or until firm.

prep + cook time
20 minutes (+ refrigeration)
makes 20

blueberry, lime and passionfruit slice

6 egg whites
1½ cups ground almonds
1½ cups confectioners' sugar
¼ cup all-purpose flour
¼ cup self-raising flour
½ cup desiccated coconut
5 ounces butter, melted
2 teaspoons finely grated lime rind
5 ounces fresh or frozen blueberries
¼ cup passionfruit pulp

1 Preheat oven to 350°F. Grease 8-inch x 12-inch rectangular pan; line base and long sides with parchment paper, extending paper 2 inches over sides.

2 Whisk egg whites in large bowl until frothy; stir in ground almonds, confectioners sugar, sifted flours, coconut, butter and rind. Pour mixture into pan; sprinkle with berries, drizzle with passionfruit.

3 Bake slice about 1¼ hours; stand slice in pan 10 minutes before turning, top-side up, onto wire rack to cool. Cut into rectangles; dust with sifted confectioners sugar to serve.

prep + cook time
1 hour 40 minutes
makes 16

choc-peanut caramel slice

Always use a premium-quality eating chocolate when baking rather than compound or any labelled light or low fat. The important thing is to use "real" chocolate, which means that it has to contain cocoa butter. If cocoa butter isn't shown on the packaging, don't buy it.

4 ounces butter, chopped
1 cup superfine sugar
12½ ounces canned sweetened condensed milk
1 cup roasted unsalted peanuts
6½ ounces dark semi-sweet chocolate, chopped coarsely
¾ ounce butter, extra

1 Grease deep 8-inch square cake pan. Fold 16-inch piece of foil lengthways into thirds; place foil strip over base and up two sides of pan (this will help lift the slice out of the pan). Line base with parchment paper.
2 Stir butter, sugar and milk in medium heavy-based saucepan over medium heat, without boiling, until sugar dissolves. Bring to the boil; boil, stirring constantly, about 10 minutes or until caramel mixture becomes a dark-honey color and starts to come away from the base and side of pan.
3 Working quickly and carefully (the mixture is very hot), pour caramel into pan; smooth with metal spatula. Press nuts into caramel with spatula. Cool 20 minutes.

4 Stir chocolate and extra butter in small heatproof bowl over small saucepan of simmering water until smooth; spread chocolate mixture over slice. Refrigerate until set. Use foil strip to lift slice from pan before cutting into squares.

prep + cook time 40 minutes (+ cooling & refrigeration) makes 40

double-chocolate slice

Slice can be stored in an airtight container for up to a week.

- 4 ounces butter, chopped coarsely
- 1 cup firmly packed dark brown sugar
- 6 ounces dark semi-sweet chocolate
- 1¼ cups rolled oats
- ¾ cup coarsely chopped walnuts
- 1 egg
- ¾ cup all-purpose flour
- ¼ cup self-raising flour
- ½ teaspoon baking soda
- ⅔ cup dark choc bits

1 Preheat oven to 325°F. Grease 8-inch x 12-inch rectangular pan; line base and long sides with parchment paper, extending paper 2 inches over sides.

2 Melt butter in medium saucepan over low heat. Remove from heat; stir in sugar until smooth.

3 Coarsely chop half the dark chocolate.

4 Stir oats and nuts into butter mixture, then egg, sifted dry ingredients, chopped chocolate and choc bits. Spread mixture evenly into pan.

5 Bake slice about 30 minutes. Cover hot slice with foil; cool.

6 Melt remaining dark chocolate. Turn slice, top-side-up, onto wire rack; drizzle with melted chocolate. Stand slice at room temperature until set before cutting.

prep + cook time 45 minutes (+ cooling & standing) makes 30

apple and prune slice

4 medium apples
¾ cup coarsely chopped
  seeded prunes
2½ cups water
½ teaspoon each ground
  cinnamon and ground
  nutmeg
2 tablespoons ground
  hazelnuts
2 sheets shortcrust pastry
1 tablespoon superfine sugar

1 Peel and core apples; slice thinly. Place apples, prunes and the water in medium saucepan; bring to the boil. Reduce heat; simmer, covered, 10 minutes or until apples are just tender. Drain well; cool 15 minutes.

2 Combine spices and ground hazelnuts in medium bowl; gently stir in apple mixture.

3 Preheat oven to 400°F. Grease 8-inch x 12-inch lamington pan; line base with parchment paper.

4 Roll one pastry sheet large enough to cover base of pan; place in pan, trim edges. Line pastry with parchment paper, fill with dried beans or rice; bake 15 minutes. Remove paper and beans; bake further 5 minutes. Spread apple mixture over pastry.

5 Roll remaining pastry sheet large enough to fit pan; place over apple filling. Brush pastry with a little water, sprinkle with sugar; score pastry in crosshatch pattern.

6 Bake slice about 45 minutes. Cool in pan; cut into squares.

prep + cook time
1 hour 30 minutes (+ cooling)
makes 24

macadamia caramel slice

Slice can be stored, refrigerated in an airtight container, for up to 4 days.

⅓ cup self-raising flour
⅓ cup all-purpose flour
¾ cup firmly packed light brown sugar
⅔ cup desiccated coconut
3 ounces butter, melted
14 ounces canned sweetened condensed milk
1 ounce butter, extra
2 tablespoons golden syrup or treacle
¾ cup coarsely chopped macadamias, roasted
1 pound white chocolate, chopped coarsely
1 tablespoon vegetable oil
pink food coloring

1 Preheat oven to 350°F. Grease 8-inch x 12-inch lamington pan; line with parchment paper, extending paper 2 inch over long sides.
2 Sift flours and sugar into medium bowl, mix in coconut and butter; press mixture evenly over base of pan. Bake 15 minutes.
3 Meanwhile, stir condensed milk, extra butter and syrup in small saucepan over medium heat about 15 minutes or until caramel mixture is golden brown.
4 Working quickly, pour caramel over base; smooth with metal spatula. Press nuts into caramel with spatula. Bake 10 minutes; cool.

5 Stir half the chocolate and half the oil in small saucepan over low heat until smooth. Pour chocolate mixture over caramel. Refrigerate 30 minutes.
6 Stir remaining chocolate and remaining oil in same cleaned pan over low heat until smooth; tint with pink food coloring. Pour pink chocolate over white chocolate. Refrigerate 2 hours. Stand slice at room temperature at least 30 minutes before cutting into squares with sharp knife.

prep + cook time 50 minutes (+ cooling & refrigeration)
makes 60

choc-cherry macaroon slice

3 egg whites

½ cup superfine sugar

3 ounces dark semi-sweet chocolate, grated coarsely

¼ cup all-purpose flour

1⅓ cups shredded coconut, toasted

¾ cup glacé cherries, chopped coarsely

1½ ounces dark semi-sweet chocolate, melted

1 Preheat oven to 300°F. Grease base of 8-inch x 12-inch rectangular pan; line base and two long sides with parchment paper, extending paper 1 inch over long sides.

2 Beat egg whites in small bowl with electric mixer until soft peaks form; gradually add sugar, beating until dissolved between additions.

3 Fold in grated chocolate, flour, coconut and cherries. Spread mixture into pan.

4 Bake slice about 45 minutes. Cool to room temperature in pan.

5 Drizzle slice with melted chocolate; refrigerate until set before cutting.

prep + cook time
1 hour (+ cooling & refrigeration)
makes 16

lemon meringue slice

It is fine to use just one 10 oz. carton of cream for this recipe.

3 ounces butter, softened
2 tablespoons superfine sugar
1 egg
1 cup all-purpose flour
¼ cup apricot jam

lemon filling
2 eggs
2 egg yolks
½ cup superfine sugar
1¼ cups pouring cream
1 tablespoon finely grated lemon rind
2 tablespoons lemon juice

meringue
3 egg whites
¾ cup superfine sugar

1 Preheat oven to 400°F. Grease base of 8-inch x 12-inch lamington pan; line base and two long sides with parchment paper, extending paper 1 inch over long sides.
2 Beat butter, sugar and egg in small bowl with electric mixer until pale in color; stir in sifted flour, in two batches. Press dough over base of pan; prick several times with fork.
3 Bake base about 15 minutes or until browned lightly. Cool 20 minutes; spread base with jam.
4 Reduce oven to 340°F.
5 Make lemon filling; pour over base.
6 Bake about 35 minutes or until set; cool 20 minutes. Roughen surface of filling with fork.

7 Increase oven to 425°F.
8 Make meringue; spread evenly over filling.
9 Bake slice about 3 minutes or until browned lightly. Cool in pan 20 minutes before cutting.

lemon filling Whisk ingredients in medium bowl until combined.

meringue Beat egg whites in small bowl with electric mixer until soft peaks form; gradually add sugar, beating until sugar dissolves.

prep + cook time
1 hour 20 minutes (+ cooling)
makes 16

dutch ginger and almond slice

1¾ cups all-purpose flour
1 cup superfine sugar
⅔ cup coarsely chopped glacé
  ginger
½ cup blanched almonds,
  chopped coarsely
1 egg
6 ounces butter, melted
2 teaspoons confectioners'
  sugar

1 Preheat oven to 350°F. Grease 8-inch x 12-inch rectangular pan; line base and long sides with parchment paper, extending paper 2 inches over sides.

2 Combine sifted flour, sugar, ginger, nuts and egg in medium bowl; stir in butter. Press mixture into pan.

3 Bake slice about 35 minutes. Stand slice in pan 10 minutes before lifting onto wire rack to cool. Dust with sifted confectioners sugar before cutting.

prep + cook time 50 minutes
makes 20

glossary

allspice also called pimento or jamaican pepper; it tastes like a combination of cumin, nutmeg, clove and cinnamon. It is available whole (pea-sized berry) or ground.

almonds

blanched whole nuts with brown skins removed.

flaked paper thin almond slices.

ground also called almond meal; nuts are powdered to a coarse flour-like texture.

baking powder a raising agent consisting mainly of two parts cream of tartar to one part baking soda.

baking soda a raising agent used in baking.

butter use salted or unsalted (sweet) butter; 4 ounces is equal to one stick of butter.

buttermilk originally the term given to the slightly sour liquid left after butter was churned from cream, today it is made similarly to yogurt. Sold alongside fresh milk products in supermarkets. Despite the implication of its name, buttermilk is low in fat.

capers the grey-green buds of a warm climate (usually Mediterranean) shrub, sold either dried and salted or pickled in a vinegar brine; baby capers are also available both in brine or dried in salt.

cardamom a spice native to India and used extensively in its cuisine; can be purchased in pod, seed or ground form. Has a distinctive aromatic, sweetly rich flavor.

cheese

cream commonly known as Philadelphia or Philly, a soft cows'-milk cheese with a fat content of at least 33%. Sold at supermarkets in bulk or in smaller-sized packages.

mascarpone an Italian fresh cultured-cream product made in much the same way as yogurt. Whiteish to creamy yellow in color, with a buttery-rich, luscious texture. Soft, creamy and spreadable, it is used in Italian desserts and as an accompaniment to fresh fruit.

chocolate

dark semi-sweet also known as luxury chocolate; made of a high percentage of cocoa liquor and cocoa butter, and a little added sugar.

milk eating the most popular eating chocolate, mild and very sweet; similar to dark with the difference being the addition of milk solids.

nonpareils small chocolate discs topped with hundreds and thousands.

peppermint cream a confectionery with a peppermint fondant center that is covered in dark chocolate.

peppermint crisp a chocolate bar with a crisp peppermint center covered with dark chocolate.

white contains no cocoa solids but derives its sweet flavor from cocoa butter. Is very sensitive to heat, so watch carefully when melting.

chocolate hazelnut spread we use Nutella in this book.

cinnamon dried inner bark of the shoots of the cinnamon tree; available in stick (quill) or ground form.

cloves dried flower buds of a tropical tree; can be used whole or in ground form. Has a distinctively pungent and 'spicy' scent and flavor.

cocoa powder also called cocoa; dried, unsweetened, roasted then ground cocoa beans (cacao seeds).

coconut

desiccated concentrated, dried, unsweetened and finely shredded coconut flesh.

flaked dried flaked coconut flesh.

shredded unsweetened thin strips of dried coconut flesh.

cookies

butternut snap crunchy cookie made with golden syrup, oats and coconut.

chocolate wheaten wheatmeal-based cookie, topped with milk or dark chocolate.

lattice an open-weave square-shaped cookie. These flaky pastry cookies are made from flour, oil, sugar and milk powder. The dough is gently rolled into very fine sheets, just like flaky pastry, and is then glazed with a light sprinkling of sugar before being baked until puffed and golden.

shortbread a pale golden, crumbly, buttery-tasting cookie made of butter, sugar and flour.

cornstarch used as a thickening agent. Available as 100% corn (maize) and wheaten cornflour.

cream
light also called fresh or pure cream. It has no additives and a minimum fat content 35%.

thick a dolloping cream with a minimum fat content of 45%.

thickened a whipping cream containing a thickener; has a minimum fat content 35%.

cream of tartar the acid ingredient in baking powder; added to confectionery mixtures to help prevent sugar from crystallising. Keeps frostings creamy and improves volume when beating egg whites.

crème fraîche a mature, naturally fermented cream (minimum fat content 35%) with a velvety texture and slightly tangy, nutty flavor. A French variation of sour cream, it can boil without curdling and can be used in sweet and savoury dishes.

cucumber, lebanese short, slender and thin-skinned. Probably the most popular variety because of its tender, edible skin, tiny, yielding seeds, and sweet, fresh and flavorsome taste.

custard powder instant mixture used to make pouring custard; it is similar to North American instant pudding mixes.

dill also called dill weed; used fresh or dried, in seed form or ground. Adds an anise/celery sweet flavor to food. Distinctive feathery, frond-like fresh leaves are grassier and more subtle than the dried version of the seeds (which slightly resemble caraway in flavor).

dried cranberries dried sweetened cranberries; commercially labelled as craisins.

eggs if recipes call for raw or barely cooked eggs, exercise caution if there is a salmonella problem in your area, particularly for children and pregnant women.

flour
plain (all-purpose) made from wheat.
rice a very fine flour made from ground white rice.

self-raising plain flour that has been sifted with baking powder in the proportion of 1 cup flour to 2 teaspoons baking powder.

wholemeal milled from whole wheat grain (bran, germ and endosperm). Available as all-purpose or self-raising.

food coloring dyes that can be used to change the color of various foods. These dyes can be eaten and do not change the taste to a noticeable extent.

gelatin if using gelatin leaves, 3 teaspoons of powdered gelatin (one sachet) is roughly equivalent to four gelatin leaves.

ginger
fresh also called green or root ginger; the thick gnarled root of a tropical plant. Can be kept, peeled, covered with dry sherry in a jar and refrigerated, or frozen in an airtight container.

glacé fresh ginger root preserved in sugar syrup; crystallized ginger (sweetened with cane sugar) can be substituted if rinsed with warm water and dried before using.

ground also called powdered ginger; used as a flavoring in cakes, pies and puddings but cannot be substituted for fresh ginger.

glacé fruit fruit such as peaches, pineapple, orange and citron that have been preserved by boiling in a heavy sugar syrup.

glucose syrup also called liquid glucose; a sugar syrup made from starches such as wheat and corn.

golden syrup a by-product of refined sugarcane; pure maple syrup or honey can be substituted.

hazelnuts also called filberts; plump, grape-size, rich, sweet nut with a brown inedible skin that is removed by rubbing heated nuts together vigorously in a tea-towel.

ground also called hazelnut meal; hazelnuts ground into a coarse or fine powder.

hundreds and thousands tiny sugar-syrup-coated sugar crystals that come in a variety of colors.

jam also called preserve or conserve; most often made from fruit.

liqueurs/spirits

coconut-flavored we used Malibu, but you can use your favorite coconut-flavored liqueur.

hazelnut-flavored we used Frangelico but you can use your favorite hazelnut-flavored liqueur.

limoncello Italian lemon-flavored liqueur; originally made from the juice and peel of lemons grown along the Amalfi coast.

rum we prefer to use an underproof rum in baking because of its more subtle flavor; however, you can use an overproof rum and still get satisfactory results.

maple syrup distilled from the sap of sugar maple trees. Most often eaten with pancakes or waffles, but also used as an ingredient in baking or in preparing desserts. Maple-flavored syrup or pancake

syrup is not an adequate substitute for the real thing.

marmalade a preserve, usually based on citrus fruit and its rind, cooked with sugar until the mixture has an intense flavor and thick consistency. Orange, lemon and lime are some of the commercially prepared varieties available.

mayonnaise we use whole-egg mayonnaise in our recipes unless stated otherwise.

milk

caramel top 'n' fill a canned milk product made of condensed milk that has been boiled to a caramel. Can be used straight from the can for cheesecakes, slices and tarts.

malted milk powder a combination of wheat flour, malt flour and milk, which are evaporated to give the powder its fine appearance and to make it easily absorbable in liquids.

sweetened condensed milk from which 60% of the water has been removed; the remaining milk is then sweetened with sugar.

mixed peel candied citrus peel.

mixed spice a blend of ground spices usually consisting of cinnamon, allspice and nutmeg.

mustard, dijon also called french. Pale brown, creamy, distinctively flavored, fairly mild french mustard.

nutmeg a strong and pungent spice ground from the dried nut of an evergreen tree native to Indonesia. Usually found ground but the flavor is more intense from a whole nut, available from spice shops, so it's best to grate your own.

oil, vegetable any of a number of oils sourced from plant rather than animal fats.

orange blossom water also called orange flower water; a concentrated flavoring made from orange blossoms. Available from Middle-Eastern food stores, some supermarkets and delis. Can't be substituted with citrus flavorings as the taste is completely different.

parchment paper also called parchment, is a silicone-coated paper that is primarily used for lining baking pans and oven trays so cakes and cookies won't stick, making removal easy.

pastry sheets packaged ready-rolled sheets of frozen puff and shortcrust (sweet and savory) pastry, available from supermarkets.

peanut butter peanuts ground to a paste; available in crunchy and smooth varieties.

peanuts not, in fact, a nut but the pod of a legume; also called ground nut.

pepitas are the pale green kernels of dried pumpkin seeds; they can be bought plain or salted.

pine nuts also known as pignoli; not a nut but a small, cream-colored kernel from pine cones. They are best roasted before use to bring out the flavor.

pistachios green, delicately flavored nuts inside hard off-white shells. Available salted or unsalted in their shells; you can also get them shelled.

pomegranate dark-red, leathery-skinned fresh fruit about the size of an orange, filled with hundreds of seeds wrapped in an edible lucent-crimson pulp having a unique tangy sweet-sour flavor.

poppy seeds small, dried, bluish-grey seeds of the poppy plant, with a crunchy texture and a nutty flavor. Can be purchased whole or ground in delicatessens and most supermarkets.

quince yellow-skinned fruit with hard texture and astringent, tart taste; eaten cooked or as a preserve. Long, slow cooking makes the flesh a deep rose pink.

rhubarb a plant with long, green-red stalks; becomes sweet and edible when cooked.

rolled oats oat groats (oats that have been husked) steamed-softened, flattened, dried and packaged as a cereal product.

rosewater distilled from rose petals, and used in the Middle East, North Africa and India to flavor desserts. Don't confuse with rose essence, which is more concentrated.

semolina coarsely ground flour milled from durum wheat; the flour used in making gnocchi, pasta and couscous.

star anise a dried star-shaped pod whose seeds have an astringent aniseed flavor; commonly used to flavor stocks and marinades.

sugar

confectioners' also known as powdered sugar; granulated sugar crushed together with a little added cornflour (cornstarch).

dark brown a moist, dark brown sugar with a rich, distinctive, full flavor coming from natural molasses syrup.

demerara a granulated, golden colored sugar with a distinctive rich flavor; often used to sweeten coffee.

granulated also known as crystal sugar; a coarse, granulated table sugar.

light brown an extremely soft, finely granulated sugar retaining molasses for its characteristic color and flavor.

pure confectioners' also known as powdered sugar, but has no added cornflour (cornstarch).

superfine also called finely granulated table sugar.

treacle a concentrated, refined sugar syrup with a distinctive flavor and dark black color.

vanilla

bean dried, long, thin pod from a tropical golden orchid; the minuscule black seeds inside the bean are used to impart a luscious vanilla flavor in baking and desserts. Place a whole bean in a jar of sugar to make the vanilla sugar; a bean can be used three or four times.

extract obtained from vanilla beans infused in water; a non-alcoholic version of essence.

watercress one of the cress family, a large group of peppery greens used raw in salads, dips and sandwiches, or cooked in soups. Highly perishable, so it must be used as soon as possible after purchase.

wheat germ the germ is where the seed germinates to form the sprout that becomes wheat. It has a nutty flavor and is very oily, causing it to turn rancid quickly, so is usually removed during milling. Available from health-food stores and supermarkets.

yogurt we use plain full-cream yogurt in our recipes unless stated otherwise.

conversion chart

measures

One Australian metric measuring cup holds about 250ml; one Australian metric tablespoon holds 20ml; one Australian metric teaspoon holds 5ml. The difference between one country's measuring cups and another's is within a two- or three-teaspoon variance, and will not affect your cooking results. North America, New Zealand and the United Kingdom use a 15ml tablespoon.

All cup and spoon measurements are level. The most accurate way of measuring dry ingredients is to weigh them. When measuring liquids, use a clear glass or plastic jug with the metric markings.

We use large eggs with an average weight of 60g.

The imperial measurements used in these recipes are approximate only.

oven temperatures

The oven temperatures in this book are for conventional ovens; if you have a fan-forced oven, decrease the temperature by 10-20 degrees.

	°F (FAHRENHEIT)	°C (CELSIUS)
Very slow	250	120
Slow	300	150
Moderately slow	325	160
Moderate	350	180
Moderately hot	400	200
Hot	425	220
Very hot	475	240

dry measures

IMPERIAL	METRIC
½oz	15g
1oz	30g
2oz	60g
3oz	90g
4oz (¼lb)	125g
5oz	155g
6oz	185g
7oz	220g
8oz (½lb)	250g
9oz	280g
10oz	315g
11oz	345g
12oz (¾lb)	375g
13oz	410g
14oz	440g
15oz	470g
16oz (1lb)	500g
24oz (1½lb)	750g
32oz (2lb)	1kg

liquid measures

IMPERIAL	METRIC
1 fluid oz	30ml
2 fluid oz	60ml
3 fluid oz	100ml
4 fluid oz	125ml
5 fluid oz (¼ pint/1 gill)	150ml
6 fluid oz	190ml
8 fluid oz	250ml
10 fluid oz (½ pint)	300ml
16 fluid oz	500ml
20 fluid oz (1 pint)	600ml
1¾ pints	1000ml (1 litre)

length measures

⅛in	3mm
¼in	6mm
½in	1cm
¾in	2cm
1in	2.5cm
2in	5cm
2½in	6cm
3in	8cm
4in	10cm
5in	13cm
6in	15cm
7in	18cm
8in	20cm
9in	23cm
10in	25cm
11in	28cm
12in (1ft)	30cm

index